Shakspere And Montaigne

Jacob Feis

Contents

I. 7
II. 11
III. 40
IV. 56
V. 117
VI. 152

SHAKSPERE AND MONTAIGNE

BY

Jacob Feis

I.
INTRODUCTION.

It has always been a daring venture to attempt finding out Shakspere's individuality, and the range of his philosophical and political ideas, from his poetical productions. We come nearest to his feelings in his 'Sonnets;' but only a few heavy sighs, as it were, from a time of languish in his life can be heard therefrom. All the rest of those lyrical effusions, in spite of the zealous exertions of commentators full of delicate sentiment and of deep thought, remain an unsolved secret.

In his historical dramas, a political creed has been pointed out, which, with some degree of certainty, may be held to have been his. From his other dramas, the most varied evidence has been drawn. A perfect maze of contradictions has been read out of them; so much so that, on this ground, we might almost despair of trustworthy results from further inquiry.

The wildest and most incongruous theories have been founded upon 'Hamlet' --the drama richest in philosophical contents. Over and over again men have hoped to be able to ascertain, from this tragedy, the great master's ideas about religion. It is well-nigh impossible to say how often such attempts have been made, but the reward of the exertions has always remained unsatisfactory. On the feelings which this masterwork of dramatic art still excites to-day--nearly three hundred years after its conception--thousands have based the most different conclusions; every one being convinced of the correctness of his own impressions.

There is a special literature, composed of such rendering of personal impressions which that most enigmatical of all dramas has made upon men of various disposition. Every hypothesis finds its adherents among a small group, whilst those who feel differently smile at the infatuation of their antagonists. Nothing that could give true and final satisfaction has yet been reached in this direction.

It is our intention to regard 'Hamlet' from a new point of view, which seems to promise more success than the critical endeavours hitherto made. We propose to enter upon a close investigation of a series of circumstances, events, and personal relations of the poet, as well as of certain indications contained in other dramatic works--all of the period in which 'Hamlet' was written and brought into publicity. This valuable material, properly arranged and put in its true connection, will, we believe, furnish us with such firm and solid stepping-stones as to allow us, on a perfectly trustworthy path, to approach the real intentions of this philosophical tragedy. It has long ago been felt that, in it, Shakspere has laid down his religious views. By the means alluded to we will now explain that credo.

We believe we can successfully show that the tendency of 'Hamlet' is of a controversial nature. In closely examining the innovations by which the augmented second quarto edition [1](1604) distinguishes itself from the first quarto, published the year before (1603), we find that almost every one of these innovations is directed against the principles of a new philosophical work-- The Essays of Michel Montaigne --which had appeared at that time in England, and which was brought out under the high auspices of the foremost noblemen and protectors of literature in this country.

From many hints in contemporary dramas, and from some clear passages in 'Hamlet' itself, it follows at the same time that the polemics carried on by Shakspere in 'Hamlet' are in most intimate connection with a controversy in which the public took a great interest, and which, in the first years of the seventeenth century, was fought out with much bitterness on the stage. The remarkable controversy is known, in the literature of that age, under the designation of the dispute between Ben Jonson and Dekker. A thorough examination of the dramas referring to it shows that Shakspere was even more implicated in this theatrical warfare than Dekker himself.

The latter wrote a satire entitled 'Satiromastix,' in which he replies to Ben Jonson's coarse personal invectives with yet coarser abuse. 'Hamlet' was Shakspere's answer to the nagging hostilities of the quarrelsome adversary, Ben Jonson, who belonged to the party which had brought the philosophical work in question into publicity. And the evident tendency of the innovations in the second quarto of 'Hamlet,' we make bold to say, convinces us that it must have been far more Shakspere's object to oppose, in that masterly production of his, the pernicious influence which the philosophy of the work alluded to threatened to exercise on the better minds of his nation, than to defend himself against the personal attacks of Ben Jonson.

The controversy itself is mentioned in 'Hamlet.' It is a disclosure of the poet, which sheds a little ray of light into the darkness in which his earthly walk is enveloped. The master, who otherwise is so sparing with allusions as to his sphere of action, speaks [2] bitter words against an 'aery of children' who were then 'in fashion,' and were 'most tyrannically clapped for it.' We are further told that these little eyases cry out on the top of the question and so berattle the common stages (so they call them), that many, wearing rapiers, are afraid of goose-quills, and dare scarce come thither.' The 'goose-quills' are, of course, the writers of the dramas played by the 'little eyases.' We then learn 'that there was for a while no money bid for argument' (Shakspere, we see, was not ashamed of honest gain) 'unless the poet and the player went to cuffs in the question.'

Lastly, the reproach is made to the nation that it 'holds it no sin to tarre them (the children) to controversy.' This satire is undoubtedly--all commentators agree upon this point--directed against the performances of the children who at that time flourished. The most popular of these juvenile actors were the Children of Paul's, the Children of the Revels, the Children of the Chapel Royal.

Shakspere's remarks, directed against these forward youngsters, may appear to us to-day as of very secondary importance in the great drama. To the poet, no doubt, it was not so. The words by which he alludes to this episode in his life come from his very heart, and were written for the purpose of reproving the conduct of the public in regard to himself.

'Hamlet' was composed in the atmosphere of this literary feud, from which we draw confirmatory proof that our theory stands on the solid ground of historical fact.
Even should our endeavour to finally solve the great problem of 'Hamlet' be made in vain, we believe we shall at least have pointed out a way on which others might be more successful. In contradistinction to the manner hitherto in use of drawing conclusions from impressions only, our own matter-of-fact attempt will have this advantage, that the time spent in it will not be wholly wasted; for, in looking round on the scene of that eventful century, we shall become more intimate with its literature and the characters of Shakspere's contemporaries.

Before entering upon the theme itself, it is necessary to cast a rapid glance at the condition of the dramatic art of that period.

Notes:
1: 'Enlarged to almost as much-againe as it was.'
2: Act ii. sc. 2.

II.

THE BEGINNINGS OF THE ENGLISH DRAMA.

THE STAGE A MEDIUM FOR POLITICAL AND RELIGIOUS CONTROVERSIES.

SHAKSPERE'S POLITICAL CREED.

FLORIO'S TRANSLATION OF MONTAIGNE'S ESSAYS.

Long before Shakspere, perhaps with fardel on his back, travelled to London, the stage, not only in the capital, but in the whole country, had begun to exercise its attractive power upon the people's imagination.

In the year 1586, a Protestant zealot, a soldier, [1] writes:--'When the belles tole to the Lectorer, the trumpetts sound to the Stages, whareat the wicked faction of Rome lawgeth for joy, while the godly weepe for sorrowe. Woe is me! the play houses are pestered when the churches are naked. At the one it is not possible to gett a place; at the other voyde seates are plentie.... Yt is a wofull sight to see two hundred proude players jett in their silks where five hundred pore people sterve in the streets.'

Already in the reign of Henry VIII. a 'Master of the Revels' was required, whose task it was to control the public representations and amusements. Queen Elizabeth had to issue several special ordinances to define more closely the functions, and provide with fresh power this office, which had been created by her father.

Like all other great achievements of the English nation, the drama, too, developed itself in this country unhampered by foreign influence. Its rapid growth was owing to the free and energetic spirit of Englishmen, to their love for public life. Every event which in some way attracted public attention, furnished the material for a new ballad, or a new drama.

Among the dramatists of that time, there was a specially active group of malcontents--men of culture, who had been at the colleges and universities; such as Peel, Greene, Marlowe, Chapman, Marston, Ben Jonson, and others. If we ask ourselves how it came about that these disciples of erudition turned over to a calling so despised in their days (for the dramatist, with few exceptions, was then mostly held in as low a repute as the player), the cause will be found in the peculiar circumstances of that epoch.

The revival of classical studies, and the art of printing, were, in the hands of the peace-loving citizen, fresh means for strengthening his position in the State. The handicraftsman or the merchant, who had gained a small fortune, was no longer satisfied with the modest prospects which he could offer to his talented son in an ordinary workshop, or in his narrow store-rooms. Since Rome no longer exercised her once all-powerful influence in every walk of life, university men, owing to their superior education, saw before them a brighter, a more hopeful, future.

In the sixteenth century the number of students in colleges and at theuniversities increased in an astonishing degree, especially from the middle classes. The sons of simple burghers entered upon the contests of free, intellectual aspirations with a zeal mostly absent in those whose position is already secured by birth. At Court, no doubt, the feudal aristocracy were yet powerful indeed. They could approach their sovereign according to their pleasure; influence him; and procure, by artful intrigue, positions of dignity and useful preferments for themselves and their favourites. Against these abuses the written word, multiplied a thousandfold, was a new weapon. Whoever could handle it properly, gained the esteem of his fellow-men; and a means was at his disposal for earning a livelihood, however scanty.

Towards the middle and the end of the sixteenth century there were many students and scholars possessing a great deal of erudition, but very little means of subsistence. Nor were their prospects very encouraging. They first went through that bitter experience, which, since then, so many have made after them--that whoever seeks a home in the realm of intellect runs the risk of losing the solid ground on which the fruits for maintaining human life grow. The eye directed towards the Parnassus is not the most apt to spy out the small tortuous paths of daily gain. To get quick returns of interest, even though it be small, from the capital of knowledge and learning, has always been, and still is, a question of difficult solution.

These young scholars, grown to manhood in the Halls of Wisdom, were unable, and even unwilling, to return to simple industrial pursuits, or to the crafty tactics of commerce. Alienated from practical activity, and too shy to take part in the harder struggles of life, many of them rather contented themselves with a crust of bread, in order to continue enjoying the 'dainties of a book.' The manlier and bolder among them, dissatisfied with the prospect of such poor fare, looked round and saw, in the hands of incapables, fat livings and lucrative emoluments to which they, on account of their superior culture, believed they had a better claim.

There were yet many State institutions which by no means corresponded to the ideal gathered from Platon, Cicero, and other writers of antiquity. Men began expressing these feelings of dissatisfaction in ballads and pamphlets. Even as the many home and foreign products of industry were distributed by commerce, so it was also the case with these new products of the intellectual workshop, which were carried to the most distant parts of the land. At the side of his other wares, the pedlar, eager for profit, offered the new and much-desired achievements of the Muse to the dwellers in the smallest village, in the loneliest farm.

Moreover, the cunning stationers had their own men, to whom they lent 'a dossen groates worth of ballads.' If these hucksters--as Henry Chettle relates--proved thrifty, they were advanced to the position of 'prety (petty) chapman,' 'able to spred more pamphlets by the State forbidden, then all the bookesellers in London; for only in this Citie is straight search, abroad smale suspition, especially of such petty pedlars.' [2]

Chettle speaks strongly against these 'intruders in the printings misserie, by whome that excelent Art is not smally slandered, the government of the State not a little blemished, nor Religion in the least measure hindred.'

Besides the profit to be derived from the Press by the malcontent travelling scholars, there was yet another way of acquiring the means of sustenance and of making use of mental culture; and in it there existed the further advantage of independence from grumbling publishers. This was the Stage. For it no great preparations were necessary, nor was any capital required. A few chairs, some boards; in every barn there was room. Wherever one man was found who could read, there were ten eager to listen.

A most characteristic drama, 'The Return from Parnassus,' depicts some poor scholars who turn away from pitiless Cambridge, of which one of them says--

> For had not Cambridge been to me unkind,
> I had not turn'd to gall a milky mind. [3]

After having long since completed their studies, they go to London to seek for the most modest livelihood. Bitter experience had taught these disciples of learning that the employment for which they waited could only be gained by bribery; and bribe they certainly could not, owing to their want of means. Some of them already show a true Werther-like yearning for solitude:--

We will be gone unto the downs of Kent....

STUDIOSO.

> So shall we shun the company of men,
> That grows more hateful as the world grows old.
> We'll teach the murm'ring brooks in tears to flow,
> And sleepy rocks to wail our passed woe. [4]

Another utters sentiments of grief, coming near the words of despair of Faust. There is a tone in them of what the Germans call Weltschmerz:--

> Curs'd be our thoughts, whene'er they dream of hope,
> Bann'd be those haps that henceforth flatter us,

When mischief dogs us still and still for aye,
From our first birth until our burying day. [5]

In the difficult choice of a calling which is to save them from need and misery, these beggar-students also think of the stage:--

And must the basest trade yield us relief?

So Philomusus, in a woebegone tone, asks his comrade Studioso; and the latter looks with the following envious words upon the players whose prospects must have been brighter and more enticing than those of the learned poor scholars:--

England affords those glorious vagabonds,
That carried erst their fardles on their backs,
Coursers to ride on through the gazing streets,
Sweeping it in their glaring satin suits,
And pages to attend their masterships:
With mouthing words that better wits have framed,
They purchase lands, and now esquires are made. [6]

Shakspere, as well as Alleyn, bought land with the money earned by their art. For many, the stage was the port of refuge to which they fled from the lonely habitations of erudition, where they--

... sit now immur'd within their private cells,
Drinking a long lank watching candle's smoke,
Spending the marrow of their flow'ring age
In fruitless poring on some worm-eat leaf. [7]

Many of these beggar students sought a livelihood by joining the players. That which the poor scholar had read and learnt in books old and new; all that he had heard from bold, adventurous warriors and seamen returning from foreign lands or recently discovered islands; in short, everything calculated to awaken interest and applause among the great mass, was with feverish haste put on the stage, and, in order to render it more palatable, mixed with a goodly dose of broad humour.

The same irreconcilable spirit of the Reformation, which would not tolerate any saint's image in the places of worship, also destroyed the liking for Miracle Plays. The tendency of the time was to turn away from mysteries and abstract notions, and to draw in art and poetry nearer to real life. Where formerly 'Miracles and Moralities' were the delight of men, and Biblical utterances, put in the mouth of prophets and saints, served to edify the audience, there the wordy warfare and the fisticuffs exchanged between the Mendicant Friar and the Seller of Indulgences [8] or Pardoner, whose profane doings were satirised on the stage, became now the subject of popular enjoyment and laughter. Every question of the day was boldly handled, and put in strong language, easily understood by the many, before a grateful public of simple taste.

The drama, thus created anew, soon became the most popular amusement in the whole country. Every other sport was forgotten over it. In every market town, in every barn, a crowd of actors met. In those days no philosophical hair-splitting was in vogue on the boards. Everything was drawn from real life; a breath of freedom pervaded all this exuberant geniality. That which a man felt to-day, tomorrow he was able to communicate to his public. The spoken word was freer than the printed one. The latter had to pass a kind of censorship; the author and the publisher could be ascertained, and be made responsible. But who would be so severe against an extemporised satirical hit, uttered perhaps by a clown? Who would, for that sake, be the denouncing traitor?

Yet it must not be thought that poets and players could do exactly as they listed. They, too, had their enemies. More especially, the austere Puritans were their bitter foes; they never ceased bringing their influence to bear upon highly-placed persons, in order to check the daring and forward doings of the stage, whose liberty they on every occasion wished to see curtailed, and its excesses visited by punishment. The ordinary players, if they did not possess licences from at least two justices of the peace, might be prosecuted, in accordance with an old law, as 'rogues and vagabonds,' and subjected to very hard sentences. It was not so easy to proceed against the better class of actors, who, with a view of escaping from the chicanery which their calling rendered them liable to, had placed themselves under the protection of the first noblemen, calling themselves their 'servants.' An ordinance of the Privy Council was required in order to bring actors who were thus protected, before a court of justice.

Nevertheless, these restless people got into incessant conflicts with the authorities. Actors would not allow themselves to be deprived of the right of saying a word on matters of the State and the Church; and what did occupy men's minds more than the victory of the Reformation?

Already, in the year 1550, Cardinal Wolsey felt bound to cast an author, Roo, [9] and 'a fellow-player, a young gentleman,' into prison, because they had put a piece on the stage, the aim of which was to show that 'Lord Governaunce (Government) was ruled by Dissipation and Negligence, by whose misgovernment and evil order Lady Public-Weal was put from Governaunce; which caused Rumor-populi, Inward Grudge, and Disdain of Wanton Sovereigntie to rise with a great multitude to expel Negligence and Dissipation, and to restore Publike-weal again to her estate--which was so done.'

The reproaches made to the bishops about the year 1544 prove, that the stage had already long ago boldly ventured upon the territory of religion, in order to imbue the masses with anti-ecclesiastical tendencies. In this connection the following words of an actor, addressed to the clerics, are most significant. 'None,' he says, 'leave ye unvexed and untroubled; no, not so much as the poor minstrels and players of interludes. So long as they played lies and sang bawdy songs, blaspheming God, and corrupting men's consciences, ye never blamed them, but were very well contented; but since they persuaded the people to worship the Lord aright, according to His holy laws and not yours, ye never were pleased with them.' [10]

The first Act of Parliament for 'the controul and regulation of stages and dramatic representations' was passed in the reign of Henry VIII. (1543). Its title is, 'An Act for the Advancement of True Religion and the Punishment of the Contrary.'

In 1552 Edward VI. issued a further proclamation both in regard to the stage and the sellers of prints and books; this time mainly from political reasons.

Whilst poets and players under Henry VIII. and his youthful successor could bring out, without hindrance, that which promoted their ideas of 'true religion,' they ran great risk, in the reign of Queen Mary, with any Protestant tendencies; for, scarcely had this severe queen been a month on the throne than she issued an ordinance (August 16, 1553) forbidding such dramas and interludes as were calculated to spread the principles and doctrines of the Reformation.

Under this sovereign, spectacles furthering the Roman Catholic cause were of course favoured. On the other hand, it may be assumed that, during the long and popular reign of Queen Elizabeth, Protestant tendencies on the stage often passed the censorship, although from the first years of her government there is an Act prohibiting any drama in which State and Church affairs were treated, 'being no meete matters to be written or treated upon but by men of authoritie, nor to be handled before any audience, but of grave and discreete persons.'

However, like all previous ordinances, proclamations, and Acts of Parliament, this one also remained without effect. The dramatists and the disciples of the mimic art continued busying themselves, in their customary bold manner, with that which awakened the greatest interest among the public at large; and one would think that at a certain time they had become a little power in the State, against which it was no longer possible to proceed in arbitrary fashion, but which, on the contrary, had to be reckoned with.

Only such measures, it appears, were afterwards passed which were calculated to harmonise the religious views uttered on the stage with the tenets of the Established Church. This follows from a letter of Lord Burleigh, addressed, in 1589, to the Archbishop of Canterbury, in which he requests him to appoint 'some fytt person well learned in divinitie.' The latter, together with the Master of the Revels and a person chosen by the Lord Mayor of the City of London, were to form a kind of Commission, which had to examine all pieces that were to be publicly acted, and to give their approval.

It would be an error to believe that this threefold censorship had any greater success than the former measures. The contrary was the case; matters rather became worse. Actors were imprisoned; whereupon they drew up beautiful petitions to their august protectors who brought about their deliverance--that is, until they were once more clapped into prison. Then they were threatened with having their ears and noses cut off; [11] but still they would not hold their tongues. We know from a letter of the French ambassador (1606)--who himself had several times to ask at the Court of James I. for the prohibition of pieces in which the Queen of France and Mademoiselle Verneuil, as well as the Duke of Biron, were severely handled--that the bold expounders of the dramatic art dared to bring their own king on the stage. Upon this there came an ordinance forbidding all further theatrical representations in London.

In the words of the French ambassador:--'I caused certain players to be forbid from acting the history of the Duke of Biron. When, however, they saw that the whole Court had left the town, they persisted in acting it; nay, they brought upon the stage the Queen of France and Mademoiselle de Verneuil…. He (the King) has upon this made order that no play shall henceforth be acted in London; for the repeal of which order they (the players) have offered 100,000 livres. Perhaps the permission will be again granted, but upon condition that they represent no recent history, nor speak of the present time.' [12]

From this sum--a very large one at that time--the importance of the theatre of those days may be gathered.

The Corporation of the City of London was among those most hostile to all theatrical representations. It exerted itself to the utmost in order to render them impossible in the centre of the capital; issuing, with that object, the most whimsical decrees. Trying, on their part, to escape from the despotic restrictions, the various players' companies settled down beyond the boundary of the Lord Mayor's jurisdiction. The citizens of London, wishing to have their share of an amusement which had become a national one, eagerly flocked to Bankside, to Blackfriars, to Shoreditch, or across green fields to the more distant Newington Butts.

Comparatively speaking, very little has come down to us from the hey-day of the English drama. That which we possess is but an exceedingly small portion of the productions of that epoch. Henslowe's 'Diary' tells us that a single theatre (Newington Butts) in about two years (June 3, 1594, to July 18, 1596) brought out not less than forty new pieces; and London, at that time, had already more than a dozen play-houses. The dramas handed down to us are mostly purged of those passages which threatened to give offence in print. The dramatists did not mean to write books. When they went to the press at all, they often excused themselves that 'scenes invented merely to be spoken, should be inforcibly published to be read.' They were well aware that this could not afford to the reader the same pleasure he felt 'when it was presented with the soule of living action.' [13]

The stage was the forum of the people, on which everything was expressed that created interest amidst a great nation rising to new life. The path towards political freedom of speech was not yet opened in Parliament; and of our important safety-valve of to-day, the public press, there was yet only the first vestige, in the shape of pamphlets secretly hawked about. The stage as rapidly decayed as it had grown, when the chief interest on which it had thriven for a while--namely, the representation of affairs of public interest--obtained more practical expression in other spheres. In the meantime, however, it remained the platform on which everything could be subjected to the criticism and jurisdiction of public opinion.

In Chettle's 'Kind-Harte's Dreame' (1592) the proprietor of a house of evil fame concludes his speech with reproaches against actors on account of their spoiling his trade; 'for no sooner have we a tricke of deceipt, but they make it common, singing jigs, and making jeasts of us, that everie boy can point out our houses as they passe by.' Again, in Ben Jonson's 'Poetaster,' we read that 'your courtier cannot kiss his mistress's slippers in quiet for them; nor your white innocent gallant pawn his revelling suit to make his punk a supper;' or that 'an honest, decayed commander cannot skelder, cheat, nor be seen in a bawdy house, but he shall be straight in one of their wormwood comedies.' [14]

Not less boldly than social affairs were political matters treated; but in order to avoid a prosecution, these questions had to be cautiously approached in parable fashion. Never was greater cleverness shown in this respect than at Shakspere's time. Every poet, every statesman, or otherwise highly-placed person, was 'heckled' under an allegorical name--a circumstance which at present makes it rather difficult for us to fully fathom the meaning of certain dramatic productions.

In order to attract the crowd, the stage-poets had to present their dishes with the condiments of actual life; thus studying more the taste of the guests than showing that of the cook. Prologues and Epilogues always appealed more to the public at large as the highest judge; its verdict alone was held to be the decisive one. Manuscripts--the property of companies whose interest it was not to make them generally known in print--were continually altered according to circumstances. Guided by the impressions of the public, authors struck out what had been badly received; whilst passages that had earned applause, remained as the encouraging and deciding factor for the future.

At one time dramas were written almost with the same rapidity as leading articles are to-day. Even as our journalists do in the press, so the dramatists of that period carried on their debates about certain questions of the day on the stage. In language the most passionate, authors fell upon each other--a practice for which we have to thank them, in so far as we thereby gain matter-of-fact points for a correct understanding of 'Hamlet.'

In the last but one decennium of the sixteenth century, the first
dramatists arose who pursued fixed literary tendencies. Often their
compositions are mere exercises of style after Greek or Roman models
which never became popular on the Thames. The taste of the English
people does not bear with strange exotic manners for any length of
time. It is lost labour to plant palm-trees where oaks only can thrive.
Lily and others endeavoured to gain the applause of the mass by words
of finely-distilled fragrance, to which no coarse grain, no breath
or the native atmosphere clung. A fruitless beginning, as little
destined to succeed as the exertions of those who tried to shine by
pedantic learning and hollow glittering words.

Marlowe's powerful imagination attempts marshalling the whole world, in
his booth of theatrical boards, after the rhythm of drumming
decasyllabon and bragging blank-verse. In his dramas, great conquerors
pass the frontiers of kingdoms with the same ease with which one steps
over the border of a carpet. The people's fancy willingly follows
the bold poet. In the short space of three hours he makes his
'Faust' [15] live through four-and-twenty years, in order 'to conquer,
with sweet pleasure, despair.' The earth becomes too small for this
dramatist. Heaven and Hell, God and the Devil, have to respond to
his inquiries. Like some of his colleagues, Marlowe is a sceptic:
he calls Moses a 'conjurer and seducer of the people,' and boasts
that, if he were to try, he would succeed in establishing a
better religion than the one he sees around himself. The apostle of
these high thoughts, not yet thirty years old, breathed his last,
in consequence of a duel in a house of evil repute.

Another hopeful disciple of lyric and dramatic poetry and prose-writer,
Robert Greene, once full of similar free-thinking ideas, lay on his
deathbed at the age of thirty-two, after a life of dissipation.
Thence he writes to his forsaken wife:--

'All my wrongs muster themselves about me; every evill at once plagues me. For my contempt of God, I am contemned of men; for my swearing and forswearing, no man will believe me; for my gluttony, I suffer hunger; for my drunkenesse, thirst; for my adulterie, ulcerous sores. Thus God has cast me downe, that I might be humbled; and punished me, for examples of others' sinne.'

Greene offers his own wretched end to his colleagues as a warning example; admonishing them to employ their 'rare wits in more profitable courses;' to look repentingly on the past; to leave off profane practices, and not 'to spend their wits in making plaies.' He especially warns them against actors--because these, it seems, had given him up. His rancorous spite against them he expresses in the well-known words:--'Yes, trust them not: for there is an upstart Crow, beautified with our feathers, that with his Tygers heart wrapt in a Players hide, supposes he is as well able to bumbast out a blank verse as the best of you; and being an absolute Johannes Fac-totum, is in his owne conceit the onely 'SHAKE-SCENE in a countrie.'

This satirical point, directed, without doubt, against Shakspere, is the only thing reliable which, down to the year 1592, we know of his dramatic activity. He had then been only about four years in London. Yet he must already have wielded considerable authority, seeing that he is publicly, though with sneering arrogance, called a complete Johannes Fac-totum--a man who has laid himself out in every direction.

It is the divine mission of a genius to bring order out of chaos, to regulate matters with the directing force of his superior glance. Certainly, Shakspere, from the very beginning of his activity, sought, with all the energy of his power, to rule out all ignoble, anarchical elements from the stage, and thus to obtain for it the sympathies of the best of his time. Fate so willed it, that one of the greatest minds which Heaven ever gave to mankind, entered, on this occasion, the modest door of a playhouse, as if Providence had intended showing that a generous activity can effect noble results everywhere, and that the most despised calling (such, still, was that of the actors then) can produce most excellent fruits.

Shakspere's life is a beneficial harmony between will and deed; no attempt to draw down Heaven to Earth, or to raise up Earth to Heaven. His are rather the ways and manners peculiar to a people which likes to adapt itself to given circumstances, to make use of the existing practical good, in order to produce from it that which is better.

It is an ascertained fact that Shakspere, who had received some training at school--but no University education--began, at the age of twenty-four, to arrange the pieces of other writers, to make modest additions to them; in short, to render them fit and proper for stage purposes. This may have been one of the causes why Greene dubbed him a 'Johannes Fac-totum.' Others, too, have accused him, during his lifetime, of 'application' (plagiarism), because he took his subjects mostly from other authors. Among those who so charged him, were, as we shall show, more especially Ben Jonson and Marston.

Shakspere never allowed himself to be induced by these reproaches to change his mode of working. Down to his death it remained the same. Is his merit, on that account, a lesser one? Certainly not: in the Poetical Art, in the Realm of Feeling and Thought, there are no regular boundary-stones. No author has the right to say: 'Thou must not step into the circle drawn by me; thou hast to do thy work wholly outside of it!'

An author who so expresses an idea, or so describes a situation as to fix it most powerfully in men's imagination, is to be looked upon as the true owner or creator of the image: to him belongs the crown.

The Greeks reckoned it to be the highest merit of the masters of their plastic art when they retained the great traits with which their predecessors had invested a conception; only endeavouring to better those parts in which a lesser success had been achieved--until that section of the work, too, had attained the highest degree of perfection. Thus arose the Jupiter of Pheidias, a Venus of Milo, an Apollo of Belvedere. Thus the noblest ideal of beauty as created, and in this wise the Greek national epic became the model of all kindred poetry.

There is a most characteristic fact which shows how greatly the drama had risen in universal esteem after Shakspere had devoted to it twelve years of his life. It is this. The Corporation of the City of London, once so hostile to all theatrical representations, and which had used every possible chicanery against the stage, had become so friendly to it towards the year 1600, that, when it was asked from governmental quarters to enforce a certain decree which had been launched against the theatre, it refused to comply with the request. On the contrary, the Lord Mayor, as well as the other magistrates, held it to be an injustice towards the actors that the Privy Council gave a hearing to the charges brought forward by the Puritans. Truly, the feelings of this conservative Corporation, as well of a large number of those who once looked down upon the stage with the greatest contempt, must, in the meanwhile, have undergone a great change.

Unquestionably the Company of the Lord Chamberlain--which in summer gave its masterly representations in the Globe Theatre, beyond the Thames, and in winter in Black-Friars--had been the chief agency in working that change. The first noblemen, the Queen herself, greatly enjoyed the pieces which Shakspere, in fact, wrote for that society; but the public at large were not less delighted with them.

When, the day after such a representation, conversation arose in the family circle as to the three happy hours passed in the theatre, an opportunity was given for discussing the most important events of the past and the present. The people's history had not yet been written then. Solitary events only had been loosely marked down in dry folios. The stage now brought telling historical facts in vivid colours before the eye. The powerful speeches of high and mighty lords, of learned bishops, and of kings were heard--of exalted persons, all different in character, but all moved, like other mortals, by various passions, and driven by a series of circumstances to definite actions. It was felt that they, too, were subject to a certain spirit of the time, the tendency of which, if the poet was attentively listened to, could be plainly gathered. In this way conclusions might be drawn which shed light even upon the events of the present.

True, it was forbidden to bring questions of the State and of religion upon the stage. But has Shakspere really avoided treating upon them?

Richard Simpson has successfully shown that Shakspere, in his historical plays, carried on a political discussion easily understood by his contemporaries. [16] The maxims thus enunciated by the poet have been ascertained by that penetrating critic in such a manner that the results obtained can scarcely be subjected to doubt any more.

On comparing the older plays and chronicles of which the poet made use for his historical dramas, with the creations that arose on this basis under his powerful hand, one sees that he suppresses certain tendencies of the subject-matter before him, placing others in their stead. Taking fully into account all the artistic technicalities calculated to produce a strong dramatic effect, we still find that he has evidently made a number of changes with the clear and most persistent intention of touching upon political questions of his time.

If, for instance, Shakspere's 'King John' is compared with the old play,

'The Troublesome Raigne,' and with the chronicles from which (but more especially from the former piece) the poet has drawn the plan of his dramatic action, it will be seen that very definite political tendencies of what he had before him were suppressed. New ones are put in their place. Shakspere makes his 'King John' go through two different, wholly unhistorical struggles: one against a foe at home, who contests the King's legitimate right; the other against Romanists who think it a sacred duty to overthrow the heretic. These were not the feuds with which the King John of history had to contend.

But the daughter from the unhappy marriage of Henry VIII. and the faithless Anne Boleyn--Queen Elizabeth--had, during her whole lifetime, to contend against rebels who held Mary Stuart to be the legitimate successor; and it was Queen Elizabeth who had always to remain armed against a confederacy of enemies who, encouraged by the Pope, made war upon the 'heretic' on the throne of England.

Thus, in the Globe Theatre, questions of the State were discussed; and politics had their distinct place there. Yet who would enforce the rules of censorship upon such language as this:--

> This England never did, and never shall,
> Lie at the proud feet of a Conqueror
> But when it first did help to wound itself.
> ... Nought shall make us rue
> If England to herself do rest but true?

Such thoughts were not taken from any old chronicle, but came from the very soul of the age that had gained the great victory over the Armada. They emphasized a newly-acquired independent position, which could only be maintained by united strength against a foreign foe.

Even as 'King John,' so all the other historical plays contain a clearly provable political tendency. Not everything done by the great queen met with applause among the people. Dissatisfaction was felt at the prominence of personal favourites, who made much abuse of commercial monopolies granted to them. The burdens of taxation had become heavier than in former times. In 'Richard the Second' a king is produced, who by his misgovernment and by his maintenance of selfish favourites loses his crown.

Shakspere's sympathies are with a prince whom Nature has formed into a strong ruler; and such an aristocrat of the intellect is depicted in his 'Henry the Fifth.' In this ideal of a king, all the good national qualities attain their apotheosis. This hero combines strength of character with justice and bravery. With great severity he examines his own conscience before proceeding to any action, however small. War he makes with all possible humanity, and only for the furtherance of civilisation. Nothing is more hated by Shakspere than a government of weak hands. From such an unfortunate cause came the Wars of the Two Roses. It seems that, in order to bring this fact home to the understanding of the people, Shakspere put the sanguinary struggles between the Houses of York and Lancaster on the stage. (See Epilogue of 'King Henry the Fifth.')

More strongly even than in his plays referring to English history, the deep aversion he felt to divided dominion pierces through his Roman tragedies; for in Shakspere the aristocratic vein was not less developed than in Goethe. To him, too, the multitude--

>...This common body,
>Like to a vagabond flag upon the stream,
>Goes to, and back, lackeying the varying tide
>To rot itself with motion. [17]

As in politics, so also in the domain of religion (of all things the most important to his contemporaries), Shakspere has made his profession of faith. For its elucidation we believe we possess a means not less sure than that which Richard Simpson has made use of for fixing the political maxims of the great master.

'Hamlet' first appeared in a quarto edition of the year 1603. The little book thus announces itself:--

'The Tragicall Historie of Hamlet Prince of Denmarke, By William Shakespeare. As it hath been diverse times acted by his Highnesse servants in the Cittie of London: as also in the two Vniversities of Cambridge & Oxford, and elsewhere.'

This drama is different, in most essential traits, from the piece we now possess, which came out a year later (1604), also in quarto edition. The title of the latter is:--

'The Tragicall Historie of Hamlet, Prince of Denmark. By William Shakespeare, Newly imprinted and enlarged to almost as much-againe as it was, according to the true & perfect coppie.'

The most diverse hypotheses have been started as to the relation between the older 'Hamlet' and the later one. [18] We share the view of those who maintain that the first quarto edition was a rough-draught, advanced to a certain degree, and for which the poet, as is the case with so many of his other plays, had used an older play as a kind of model. A 'rough-draught advanced to a certain degree' may be explained as a piece already produced on the stage. The public, always eager to see novelties, allowed the dramatists little time for fully working out their conceptions. The plays matured, as it were, on the stage itself; there they received their final shape and completion. As mentioned before, that which had displeased was struck out, whilst the passages that had obtained applause were often augmented, in order to confer upon the play the attraction of novelty. 'Enlarged to almost as much-againe as it was' is an expression which shows that 'Hamlet' had drawn from the very beginning. The poet, thereby encouraged, then worked out this drama into the powerful, comprehensive tragedy which we now possess.

Now, in closely examining the changes and additions made in the second 'Hamlet,' we find that most of the freshly added philosophical thoughts, and many characteristic peculiarities, have clear reference to the philosophy of a certain book and the character of its author--namely, to Michel Montaigne and his 'Essais.' This work first appeared in an English translation in 1603, after it had already been entered at Stationers' Hall for publication in 1599. The cause which may have induced Shakspere to confer upon his 'Hamlet' the thoughts and the peculiarities of Montaigne, and to give that play the shape in which we now have it, will become apparent when we have to explain the controversy between Jonson and Dekker. We have thus the advantage over Simpson's method, that our theory will be confirmed from other sources.

Montaigne's 'Essais' were a work which made a strong mark, and created a deep sensation, in his own country. There, it had already gone through twelve editions before it was introduced in England--eleven years after the death of its author--by means of a translation. Here it found its first admirers among the highest aristocracy and the patrons of literature and art. Under such august auspices it penetrated into the English public at large. The translator was a well-known teacher of the Italian language, John Florio.

From the preface of the first book of the 'Essais' we learn that, at the request of Sir Edward Wotton, Florio had first Englished one chapter, doing it in the house of Lady Bedford, a great lover of art.

In that preface, Florio, in most extravagant and euphuistic style, describes how this noblewoman, after having 'dayned to read it (the first chapter) without pitty of my fasting, my fainting, my laboring, my langishing, my gasping for some breath ... yet commaunded me on'--namely, to turn the whole work into English. It was a heavy task for the poor schoolmaster. He says:--'I sweat, I wept, and I went on sea-tosst, weather-beaten ... shippe-wrackt--almost drowned.' 'I say not,' the polite maestro adds, 'you took pleasure at shore' (as those in this author, iii. 1). No; my lady was 'unmercifull, but not so cruell;' she ever and anon upheld his courage, bringing 'to my succour the forces of two deare friends.' One of them was Theodore Diodati, tutor of Lady Bedford's brother, the eldest son of Lady Harrington whose husband also was a poet.

The grateful Florio calls this worthy colleague, 'Diodati as in name, so indeed God's gift to me,' and a 'guide-fish' who in this 'rockie-rough ocean' helped him to capture the 'Whale'--that is, Montaigne. He also compares him to a 'bonus genius sent to me, as the good angel to Raimond in "Tasso," for my assistant to combat this great Argante.'

The other welcome fellow-worker was 'Maister Doctor Guinne;' according to Florio, 'in this perilous, crook't passage a monster-quelling Theseus or Herkules;' aye, in his eyes the best orator, poet, philosopher, and medical man (non so se meglior oratore e poeta, o philosopho e medico), and well versed in Greek, Latin, Italian, and French poetry. It was he who succeeded in tracing the many passages from classic and modern writers which are strewn all over Montaigne's Essays to the divers authors, and the several places where they occur, so as to properly classify them.

Samuel Daniel, a well-known and much respected poet of that time, and a brother-in-law of Florio, also made his contribution. He opens this powerful, highly important work with a eulogistic poem. Florio, in his bombastic style, says:--'I, in this, serve but as Vulcan to hatchet this Minerva from that Jupiter's bigge braine.' He calls himself 'a fondling foster-father, having transported it from France to England, put it in English clothes, taught it to talke our tongue, though many times with a jerke of French jargon.'

The 'Essais' consist of three different books. Each of them is dedicated to two noblewomen, the foremost of this country. The first book isdedicated to Lucy, Countess of Bedford, and her mother, Lady Anne Harrington. The second to Elizabeth, Countess of Rutland, daughter of the famous poet Sir Philip Sidney, therefore a near relation of Shakspere's youthful friend, William Herbert, the later Earl of Pembroke ('the only begetter' of the 'Sonnets'), whose mother also was a daughter of that much-admired poet.

The second book is dedicated to the renowned as well as evilly notorious Lady Penelope Rich, sister of the unfortunate Earl of Essex. She shone by her extraordinary beauty as well as by her intellectual gifts. Of her Sir Philip Sidney was madly enamoured, but she married a Croesus, Lord Rich. This union was a most unhappy one. Her husband, a man far below her in strength of mind, did not know how to value the jewel that had come into his possession. A crowd of admirers flocked around her, among whom was William Herbert, much younger in years than herself. It is suspected that Shakspere's last sonnets (127-152) touch upon this connection, with the object of warning the friend against the true character of that sinful woman.

The last book is dedicated to Lady Elizabeth Grey, the wife of Henry Grey, daughter of the Earl of Shrewsbury, and to Lady Mary Nevill, the latter being the daughter of the Chancellor of the Exchequer, and wife of Sir Henry Nevill of Abergavenny.

Each of the noblewomen mentioned is praised in a sonnet. No book of that period had such a number of aristocratic sponsors. Yet it was of foreign origin, and for the first time a French philosopher had appeared in an English version on this side of the Channel. His easy, chatty tone must have created no small sensation. The welcome given to him by a great number of men is proved by the fact of the 'Essais' soon reaching their third edition, a rare occurrence with a book so expensive as this. [19]

We will endeavour to sketch the character of Michel Montaigne and his writings. His individuality, owing to the minute descriptions he gives of his own self in the Essays, comes out with rare distinctness from the dark environs of his time--more clearly so than the personality of any other author, even of that seventeenth century which is so much nearer to us.

This French nobleman devoted the last thirty years of his life to philosophical speculations, if that expression is allowable; for fanciful inclination and changing sentiment, far more than strict logic and sound common sense, decided the direction of his thoughts. The book in which he tries to render his ideas is meant to be the flesh and blood of his own self. The work and the author--so he says--are to be one. 'He who touches one of them, attacks both.' In the words of Florio's translation, he observes:--'Authors communicate themselves unto the world by some speciall and strange marke, I the first by my generall disposition as Michael Montaigne; not as a Grammarian, or a Poet, or a Lawyer.'

Few writers have been considered from such different points of view as Montaigne. The most passionate controversies have arisen about him. Theologians have endeavoured to make him one of their own; but the more far seeing ones soon perceived that there was too much scepticism in his work. Some sceptics would fain attach him to their own ranks;

but the more consistent among them declined the companionship of one who was too bigoted for them. The great mass of men, as usual, plucked, according to each one's taste and fancy, some blossom or leaf from his 'nosegay of strange flowers,' [20] and then classified him from that casual selection.

Montaigne, a friend of truth, admonishes posterity, if it would judge him, to do so truthfully and justly. With gladsome heart, he says, he would come back from the other world in order to give the lie to those who describe him different from what he is, 'even if it were done to his honour.'

We shall strive to comply with his wish by drawing the picture of this most interesting, and in his intellectual features thoroughly modern, man, from the contours furnished by his own hand. We shall exert ourselves to lay stress on those characteristics by which he must have created most surprise among his logically more consistent contemporaries on the other side of the Channel.

In taking up Montaigne's 'Essais' for perusal we are presently under the spell of a feeling as though we were listening to the words of a most versatile man of the world, in whom we become more and more interested. We find in him not only an amiable representative of the upper classes, but also a man who has deeply entered into the spirit of classic antiquity. Soon he convinces us that he is honestly searching after truth; that he pursues the noble aim of placing himself in harmony with God and the world. Does he succeed in this? Does he arrive at a clear conclusion? What are the fruits of his thoughts? what his teachings? In what relation did he stand to his century?

As in no other epoch, men had, especially those who came out into the fierce light of publicity, to take sides in party warfare during the much-agitated time of the Reformation. To which party did Montaigne belong? Was he one of the Humanists, who, averse to all antiquated dogmas, preached a new doctrine, which was to bring mankind once more into unison with the long despised laws of Nature?

We hope to show successfully that Shakspere wrote his 'Hamlet' for the great and noble object of warning his contemporaries against the disturbing inconsistencies of the philosophy of Montaigne who preached the rights of Nature, whilst yet clinging to dogmatic tenets which cannot be reconciled with those rights.

We hope to prove that Shakspere who made it his task 'to hold the mirror up to Nature,' and who, like none before him, caught up her innermost secrets, rendering them with the chastest expression; that Shakspere, who denied in few but impressive words the vitality of any art or culture which uses means not consistent with the intentions of Nature:

> Yet Nature is made better by no mean,
> But Nature makes that mean; so o'er that art
> Which, you say, adds to Nature, is an art
> That Nature makes; [21]--

we hope to prove successfully that Shakspere, this true apostle of Nature, held it to be sufficient, ay, most godly, to be a champion of 'natural things;' that he advocated a true and simple obedience to her laws, and a renunciation of all transcendental dogmas, miscalled 'holy and reverent,' which domineer over human nature, and hinder the free development of its nobler faculties.

Let us then impartially examine the character and the work of Montaigne. If we discover contradictions in both, we shall not endeavour to argue them away, but present them with matter-of-fact fidelity; for it is on those very contradictions that the enigmatic, as yet unexplained, character of Hamlet reposes.

Notes:
1: Collier's Drama, i. 265.
2: Kind-hartes Dreame, 1592.
3: Act v. sc. 4.
4: Act v sc. 4.
5: Act iii sc. 5.
6: The Return from Parnassus, act v. sc. I.
7: Ibid., act iv. sc. 3.
8: The Pardoner and the Friar: 1533.
9: Collier's Drama, i. 104.
10: The Political Use of the Stage in Shakspere's Time.
New Shakspere Society: 1874, ii. p. 371.
Henry Stalbrydge, Epistle Exhortatory, &c.: 1544.
11: This threat was uttered against Chapman, Ben Jonson, and Marston on account of Eastward Hoe.
12: Von Raumer, ii. p. 219.
13: Marston's Malcontent: Dedication.
14: Act i. sc. I.
15: It is very characteristic that, in this serious piece also, low humour was still largely employed. In printing--the publisher remarks--the passages in question were left out, as derogatory 'to so honourable and stately a history.'
16: The Politics of Shakspere's Historical Plays. New Shakspere Society, ii. 1874.
17: Antonius and Cleopatra, act i. sc. 4.
18: We mean the usually received text, seeing that the folio edition of 1623 contains some passages which are wanting in the quarto edition, and vice versa.
19: Montaigne's Essays, which were published in folio, may have had the same price as Shakspere's folio of 1623. The latter was only

re-issued in 1632 and 1664, whilst the former came out in new editions in 1613 and 1632.

20: 'Icy un amas de fleur estrangieres, n'y ayant fourny du mien que le filet a les lier' (iii. 12).

21: Winter's Tale, act iv. sc. 3.

III.
MONTAIGNE.

Michel Montaigne was favoured by birth as few writers have been. He was the son of a worthy nobleman who gave him, from early childhood, a most carefully conducted education. He never tires in praising the good qualities of his father, who had followed Francis I. to his Italian campaigns, and, like that monarch, had conceived a preference for those classical studies which were then again reviving. Even as his king, he, too, wished to promote the new knowledge, and was bent upon so initiating young Michel into it as to make him in the fullest manner conversant with the conquests of Greece and Rome in the realm of intellect.

In this, as a practical man who felt the greatest respect for erudition without personally possessing a proper share of it, he allowed himself to be thoroughly guided by 'men of learning and judgment.' He had been told that the only reason why we do not 'attain to the greatness of soul and intellect of the ancient Greeks and Romans was the length of time we give to learning these languages which cost them nothing.' In bringing up the boy, to whom the best masters were given, the procedures chosen were therefore such that young Michel, in his sixth year, spoke Latin thoroughly before he was able to converse in his own mother-tongue.

Montaigne relates [1] that he was much more at home on the banks of the Tiber than on the Seine. Before he knew the Louvre, his mind's eye rested on the Forum and the Capitol. He boasts of having always been more occupied with the life and the qualities of Lucullus, of Metellus, and Scipio, than with the fate of any of his own countrymen. Of the hey-day of classic Rome he, who otherwise uses such measured terms, speaks with a glowing enthusiasm. He often avers that he belongs to no special school of thought; that he advocates no theory; that he is not the adherent of any party or sect. To him--so he asserts--an unprejudiced examination of all knowledge is sufficient. His endeavour was, to prove the devise of his escutcheon: 'Que scais-je?'

Have the humanistic studies not given to him, as to so many of his contemporaries, a distinctive mental bent? Have Greek and Roman philosophy and poetry remained without any influence upon him? Has his character not been formed by them? Does he not once reckon himself among 'nous autres naturalistes?' [2]

Once only, it is true, he does this; but even if he who would not belong to any special school of thought, and who would rather be 'a good equerry than a logician,' [3] had not ascribed to himself this designation, a hundred passages of his work would bear witness to the fact of his having been one of the Humanists, on whose banner 'Nature' was written as the parole. Ever and anon he says (I here direct attention more specially to his last Essays) that we ought willingly to follow her prescriptions; and incessantly he asserts that, in doing so, we cannot err. He designates her as a guide as mild as she is just, whose footprints, blurred over as they are by artificial ones, we ought everywhere to trace anew. 'Is it not folly,' he asks with Seneca, [4] 'to bend the body this way, and the mind that way, and thus to stand distorted between two movements utterly at variance with each other?'

To bring up and to guide man in accordance with his capacities, is with him a supreme law. 'Le glorieux chef-d'oeuvre de l'homme, c'est de vivre a propos.' He, the sage, is already so much in advance of his century that he yearns for laws and religions which are not arbitrarily founded, but drawn from the roots and the buds of a universal Reason, contained in every person not degenerate or divorced from nature desnature. A mass of passages in the Essays strengthen the opinion that Montaigne was an upright, noble-minded Humanist, a disciple of free thought, who wished to fathom human nature, and was anxious to help in delivering mankind from the fetters of manifold superstitions. Read his Essay on Education; and the conviction will force itself upon you that in many things he was far in advance of his time.

But now to the reverse of the medal--to Montaigne as the adherent of Romanist dogmas!

'The bond,' he says--and here we quote Florio's translation, [5] only slightly changed into modern orthography--'which should bind our judgment, tie our will, enforce and join our souls to our Creator, should be a bond taking his doublings and forces, not from our considerations, reasons, and passions, but from a divine and supernatural compulsion, having but one form; one countenance, and one grace; which is the authority and grace of God.' The latter, be it well understood, are to Montaigne identical with the Church of Rome, to which he thinks it best blindly to submit.

Men--he observes--who make bold to sit in judgment upon their judges, are never faithful and obedient to them. As a warning example he points to England, which, since his birth, had already three or four times changed its laws, not only in matters political, in which constancy is not insisted upon, but in the most important matter imaginable--namely, in religion. He declares himself all the more ashamed of, and vexed by, this, as his own family were allied by close private ties with the English nation.

An attempt has been made to show [6] that in Montaigne's 'Apologie de Raymond Sebond,' in which he expounds his theological opinions in the most explicit manner, a hidden attack is contained upon the Church. But it bespeaks an utter misconception of the character of this writer to hold him capable of such perfidious craftiness; for he calls it 'a cowardly and servile humour if a man disguises and hides his thoughts under a mask, not daring to let himself be seen under his true aspect.' [7]

We know of not a few, especially Italian, Humanists who publicly made a deep bow before the altar, whilst behind it they cynically laughed, in company with their friends; making sport of the silly crowd that knelt down in profound reverence. Montaigne was no such double-dealer. We can fully believe him when he states that it is to him no small satisfaction and pleasure to 'have been preserved from the contagion of so corrupt an age; to have never brought affliction and ruin upon any person; not to have felt a desire for vengeance, or any envy; nor to have become a defaulter to his word.' [8]

His word, his honour, were to him the most sacred treasure. He never would have descended so low as to fling them to the winds. Let us, therefore, not endeavour to deny any logical inconsistencies in his writings--inconsistencies which many other men since his time have equally shown. Let us rather institute a strict and close inquiry into these two modes of thought of his, which, contradictory as they are, yet make up his very character and individuality.

We can fully believe in Montaigne's sincerity when elsewhere he asserts that we must not travel away from the paths marked down by the Roman Catholic Church, lest we should be driven about helplessly and aimlessly on the unbounded sea of human opinions. He tells us [9] that 'he, too, had neglected the observance of certain ceremonies of the Church, which seemed to him somewhat vain and strange; but that, when he communicated on that subject with learned men, he found that these things had a very massive and solid foundation, and that it is only silliness and ignorance which make us receive them with less reverence than the other doctrines of religion.' Hence he concludes that we must put ourselves wholly under the protection of ecclesiastical authority, or completely break with it.

He never made a single step to withdraw himself from that authority. He rather prides himself on having never allowed himself, by any philosophy, to be turned away from his first and natural sic opinions, and from the condition in which God had placed him; being well aware of his own variability volubilite. 'Thus I have, by the grace of God, remained wholly attached, without internal agitation and troubles of conscience, to the ancient beliefs of our religion, during the conflict of so many sects and party divisions which our century has produced.' [10]

Receiving the holy Host, he breathed his last.

In the 'Apologie de Raymond Sebond,' Montaigne defends the 'Theologia Naturalis' of the latter--a book in which the author, who was a medical man, a philosopher, and a theologian, endeavours to prove that the Roman Catholic dogmas are in harmony with the laws of nature. That which is to be received in full faith, Sebond exerts himself to make comprehensible by arguments of the reason. This book--so Montaigne relates--had been given to his father, at the time when Luther's new doctrines began to be popular, by a man of great reputation for learning, Pierre Bunel, who 'well foresaw, by his penetration, [11] that this budding disease would easily degenerate into an execrable atheism.' Old Pierre Montaigne, a very pious man, esteemed this work very highly; and a few days before his death, having fortunately found it among a lot of neglected papers, commanded his son to translate it from 'that kind of Spanish jargon with Latin endings,' in which it was written.

Michel, with filial piety, fulfilled his task. He translated the work, and in the above-mentioned Essay--the largest of the series--he advocates its philosophy. The essence of this panegyric of the Church (for logic would in vain be sought for in that Essay) is: that knowledge and curiosity are simply plagues of mankind, and that the Roman Catholic religion, therefore, with great wisdom, recommends ignorance. Man would be most likely to attain happiness if, like the animal, he were to allow himself to be guided by his simple instinct. All philosophising is declared to be of no use. Faith only is said to afford security to the weakest of all beings, to man, who more than any other creature is exposed to the most manifold dangers. No elephant, no whale, or crocodile, was required to overcome him who proudly calls himself the 'lord of creation.' 'Little lice are sufficient to make Sylla give up his dictatorship. The heart and the life of a mighty and triumphant emperor form but the breakfast of a little worm.' [12] (Compare 'Hamlet,' iv. 3).

Montaigne, who, in his thirty-eighth year, 'long weary of the bondage of Court and of public employment, while yet in the vigour of life, hath withdrawn himself into the bosom of the Learned Virgins (Doctarum Virginum),' [13] so as to be able to spend the rest of his days in his ancestral home, in peaceful, undisturbed devotion to ennobling studies, and to present the world with a new book, in which he means to give expression to his innermost thoughts--Montaigne, in his Essay 'On Prayers,' calls his writings 'rhapsodies,' which he submits to the judgment of the Church, so that it may deal with anything he, 'either ignorantly or unadvisedly, may have set down contrary to the sacred decrees, and repugnant to the holy prescriptions of the Catholic, Apostolic, and Roman Church, wherein I die, and in which I was born.'

Let us not dwell too long on the contradictions of a man who professes to think independently, and who yet is content with having a mind-cramping dogmatic creed imposed upon him. Let us look at a few other, not less irreconcilable, inconsistencies of his logic.

Montaigne, the Humanist, advocates toleration. Justice, he says, is to be done to every party, to every opinion. 'Men are different in feeling and in strength; they must be directed to their good, according to themselves, and by diverse ways.' [14] He bears no grudge to anyone of heterodox faith; he feels no indignation against those who differ from him in ideas. The ties of universal humanity he values more than those of national connection. He has some good words for the Mexicans, so cruelly persecuted by the Spaniards. 'I hold all men to be my compatriots; I feel the same love for a Pole as for a Frenchman.' [15]

But when we read what the Roman Catholic Montaigne writes, there is a different tone:--

'Now that which, methinks, brings so much disorder into our consciences--namely, in these troubles of religion in which we are--is the easy way with which Catholics treat their faith. They suppose they show themselves properly moderate and skilful when they yield to their adversaries some of the articles that are under debate. But--besides that they do not see what an advantage it is to your antagonist if you once begin making a concession, thus encouraging him to follow up his point--it may further be said that the articles which they choose as apparently the lightest, are sometimes most important indeed.' [16]

Again, the humane nobleman who looks with pity and kindliness upon 'the poor, toiling with heads bent, in their hard work;' he who calls the application of the torture 'a trial of patience rather than of truth'--he maintains that 'the public weal requires that one should commit treachery, use falsehoods, and perform massacres.' [17]

Personally, he shrinks from such a mission. His softer heart is not strong enough for these deeds. He relates [18] that he 'never could see without displeasure an innocent and defenceless beast pursued and killed, from which we have received no offence at all.' He is moved by the aspect of 'the hart when it is embossed and out of breath, and, finding its strength gone, has no other resource left but to yield itself up to us who pursue it, asking for mercy from us by its tears. He calls this 'a deplorable spectacle.'

Yet, this sentimental nobleman advocates the commission of treachery and cruelty, in the interest of the State, by certain more energetic, less timorous men. Nor does he define their functions so as to raise a bar against a second St. Bartholomew massacre. A deed of this kind he would submissively take to be an act of Heaven, shirking all responsibility for, or discussion of, anything that 'begins to molest him.' He merely says:--'Like those ancients who sacrificed their lives for the welfare of their country, so they (the guardians of the State) must be ready to sacrifice their honour and their conscience. We who are weaker, take easier, less risky parts.' [19]

In Montaigne, the Humanist, we read that beautiful passage (in his last Essay [20]) where he says that 'those who would go beyond human nature, trying to transform themselves into angels, only make beasts of themselves.' [21] Yet, elsewhere [22] he writes that he shall be exalted, who, renouncing his own natural means, allows himself to be guided by means purely celestial--by which he clearly understands the dogmas of Roman Catholicism.

As a humanistic thinker, Montaigne fears nothing more than any strivings after transcendentalism. Such yearnings terrify him like inaccessible heights. In the life of Sokrates, of that sage for whom he felt a special preference, the 'ecstasies and daimons' greatly repel him. Nevertheless, Montaigne, the mystic, attributes a great magic power to such daimons;

for he says: 'I, too, have sometimes felt within myself an image of such internal agitations, as weak in the light of reason as they were violent in instinctive persuasion or dissuasion (a state of mind more ordinary to Sokrates), by which I have so profitably, and so happily, suffered myself to be drawn on, that these mental agitations might perhaps be thought to contain something of divine inspiration.' [23]

Montaigne, the admirer of classic antiquity, says that serving the Commonwealth is the most honourable calling. [24] Acts without some splendour of freedom have, in his eyes, neither grace, nor do they merit being honoured. [25] But elsewhere [26] we come upon his other view, less imbued with the spirit of antiquity--namely, that 'man alone, without other help, armed only with his own weapons, and unprovided with the grace and knowledge of God, in which all his honour, his strength, and the whole ground of his being are contained,' is a sorry specimen of force indeed. His own reason gives him no advantage over other creatures; the Church alone confers this privilege upon him!

During several years, Montaigne was Mayor of Bordeaux. With great modesty, he relates [27] that in his mere passive conduct lay whatever little merit he may have had in serving his town. This fully harmonises with the view expressed in his last but one Essay, in which he declares that we are to be blamed for not sufficiently trusting in Heaven; expecting from ourselves more than behoves us: 'Therefore do our designs so often miscarry. Heaven is envious of the large extent which we attribute to the rights of human wisdom, to the prejudice of its own rights; and it curtails ours all the more that we endeavour to enlarge them.' [28]

Montaigne by no means ignores the troublous character of the times in which he lived. He often alludes to it. He thinks astrologers cannot have any great difficulty in presaging changes and revolutions near at hand:--'Their prophetic indications are practically in our very midst, and most palpable; one need not search the Heavens for that.'

'Cast we our eyes about us' (here again we follow Florio's translation), 'and in a generall survay consider all the world: all is tottring; all is out of frame. Take a perfect view of all great states, both in Christendome and where ever else we have knowledge of, and in all places you shall finde a most evident threatning of change and ruine ... Astrologers may spout themselves, with warning us, as they doe of iminent alterations and succeeding revolutions: their divinations are present and palpable, we need not prie into the heavens to find them out.' [29]

But Montaigne, always resigned to the will of God, inactively stands by. Not even a manly counsel comes from his lips. He believes he has fulfilled his Christian duty by trusting in Heaven for the conduct of human affairs, and trying to comfort his fellow-men by the hollow words that he 'sees no cause for despair. Perchance we have not yet arrived at the last stage. The maintenance of states is most probably something that goes beyond our powers of understanding.' [30]

Montaigne, the Humanist, says that 'it is an absolute perfection, and, as it were, a divine accomplishment for a man to know how to loyally enjoy his existence.' The most commendable life for him is 'that which adapts itself, in an orderly way, to a common human model, without miracle, and without extravagance.' [31]

But Montaigne, the Christian, relates that he has 'never occupied himself with anything more than with ideas of death, even at the most licentious time of his youth.' With touching ingenuousness he confesses his weaknesses and his vanities, of which he scarcely dares to think any longer. The descriptions he often gives of himself--such as, 'a dreamer' (songe-creux), 'soft' (molle), 'heavy' (poisante), 'pensive,' and so forth [32]--prove that he cannot have arrived at a pure enjoyment of life. He questions the happiness of being a husband and father. We shall touch upon his views as regards woman, and many other peculiarities of his, in the passages of 'Hamlet' referring to them.

In nothing does Montaigne arrive at any clear conclusion within himself. Though he knows how to speak much and well about everything, it is all mere bel esprit, a display of glittering words, hollow verbiage, which only lands us in a labyrinth of contradictions, from which we seek an issue as vainly as the author himself. Striving, through all his life, to arrive at a knowledge of himself, he at last lays down his arms, considering the attempt a fruitless and impossible task, and, in his last Essay, [33] he makes this avowal:--

'That which in Perseus, the King of Macedon, was remarked as a rare thing--viz. that his mind, not settling down into any kind of condition, went wandering through every manner of life, thus showing such flighty and erratic conduct that neither he nor others knew what sort of man he was: this seems to me to apply nearly to the whole world, and more especially to one of that ilk whom this description would eminently fit. This, indeed, is what I believe of him (he speaks of himself):--"No average attitude; being always driven from one extreme to the other by indivinable chances; no manner of course without cross-runnings and marvellous controversies; no clear and plain faculty, so that the likeliest idea that could one day be put forth about him will be this: that he affected and laboured to make himself known by the impossibility of really knowing him" ('qu'il affectoit et estudioit de se rendre cogneu par estre mecognoissable').' This is Montaigne all over.

In the British Museum there is a copy of the Essays of Montaigne, in Florio's translation, with Shakspere's name, it is alleged, written in it by his own hand, and with notes which possibly may in part have been jotted down by him. Sir Frederick Madden, one of the greatest authorities in autographs, has recognised Shakspere's autograph as genuine. [34] Whatever disputes may be carried on on this particular point, we think we shall be able to prove that Shakspere about the year 1600 must have been well acquainted with Montaigne. We shall show that in the first text of 'Hamlet,' which, it is assumed, was represented on the stage between 1601 and 1602, there are already to be found some allusions to Montaigne, especially as far as the middle of the second and towards the end of the fifth act. In all likelihood, Shakspere knew the 'Essais' even in the original French text or perhaps from the manuscript of the translation which, as above stated, had been begun towards the year 1599; for Shakspere, it is to be supposed, had access to the houses of, at least, two of the noble ladies to whom the Italian teacher dedicated his translation.

In the 'Tempest,' assumed to be of later date than 'Hamlet,' there is a passage unmistakably taken from Florio's version of Montaigne. [35]

Ben Jonson, the most quarrelsome and the chief adversary of Shakspere, was an intimate friend of Florio. When Montaigne, in 'Hamlet'--as Jonson says--became the target of 'railing rhetoric,' the latter took sides with Florio and his colleagues; launching out against Shakspere in his comedy, 'Volpone.' This play, as well as an Introduction in which it is dedicated to the two Universities, gives us a clue to a great many things otherwise difficult to understand.

A new book, especially a philosophical work like that of Michel Montaigne, was then still a remarkable event. [36] To counteract the pernicious influence which the frivolous, foreign talker threatened to exercise, in large circles, through an English translation--this, in our opinion, was the object which Shakspere had when touching upon ground interdicted, as a rule, to the stage--namely, upon questions of religion. We shall find that it was not through any preference for ghost and murder scenes that, a year after the second quarto, in 1605, 'Hamlet' was reprinted--a circumstance occurring with but one other drama of Shakspere; which testifies that this particular play attained great popularity from its first appearance. [37]

A very instructive insight into the intellectual movement of the great Reformation epoch here opens itself to us. In this case, also, we shall gain the conviction that a true genius takes the liveliest interest in the fate of his own nation, and does not occupy himself with distant, abstruse problems (such as fussy metaphysicians would fain philosophise into 'Hamlet'), whilst the times are going out of joint. The greatest Englishman remained, in the most powerful drama of his, within the sphere of the questions that agitated his time. In 'Hamlet' he identifies Montaigne's philosophy with madness; branding it as a pernicious one, as contrary to the intellectual conquests his own English nation has made, when breaking with the Romanist dogmas.

What sense of duty do Montaigne's Essays promote? What noble deed can ripen in the light of the disordered and discordant ideas they contain? All they can do is, to disturb the mind, not to clear it; to give rise to doubts, not to solve them; to nip the buds from which great actions may spring, not to develop them. Instead of furthering the love for mankind, they can only produce despair as to all higher aims and ideals.

In 'Hamlet,' Shakspere personified many qualities of the complex character of Montaigne. Before all, he meant to draw this conclusion: that whoever approaches a high task of life with such wavering thoughts and such logical inconsistencies, must needs suffer shipwreck. Hamlet's character has only remained an enigma to us for so long a time because he is flesh of our flesh, blood of our blood; 'but, to knew a man well, were to know himself.'

Notes:
1: Essay III. 9.
2: Essay III. 12, 235.
3: Ibid. 9.
4: Essay III. 13 (Edition Variorum, par Charles Louandre, Paris; which we always refer to).
5: The Essayes, or Morall, Politike, and Millitarie Discourses of Lo. Michaell de Montaigne, London, 1603, p. 256.
6: Sainte-Beuve.
7: Essay II. 17, p. 71.
8: III. 2, 330.
9: Essay I. 26, 257.
10: II. 12, 487-8.
11: Montaigne, Discours de Raison (Discourse of Reason). Florio, 252.
12: Essay II. 12, 297. Florio, 266.
13: Part of an inscription still legible in Montaigne's castle.
14: Essay II. 12.
15: III. 9.
16: I. 26.
17: Essay III. 1
18: II. 11.
19: III. 1.
20: III. 13.
21: Essay III. 13.
22: II. 12.
23: I. 11.
24: III. 9.
25: Ibid.
26: II. 12.
27: Essay III. 10.
28: Ibid. 12.
29. Florio, 575.

30: Essay III. 9.
31: III. 13.
32: Essay II. 12.
33: III. 13.
34: Observations on an Autograph of Shakspere. London, 1838.
35: This is the passage, which occurs in the Tempest, act ii. sc. I:

'Gonzalo.--I' the commonwealth I would by contraries
Execute all things: for no kind of traffic
Would I admit; no name of magistrate:
Letters should not be known; riches, poverty,
And use of service, none; contract, succession,
Bourn, bound of land, tilth, vineyard, none;
No use of metal, corn, or wine, or oil;
No occupation: all men idle, all;
And women too.'

This passage is almost literally taken from Essay I. 30, 'On Cannibals.' We shall later on show Shakspere's reason for giving us this fanciful description of such an Utopian commonwealth.

36: Florio, after enumerating the difficulties he encountered in the translation of the Essays, concludes his preface to the courteous reader with the following words:--

'In summe, if any think he could do better, let him trie, then will he better think of what is done. Seven or eight of great wit and worth have assayed, but found those Essais no attempt for French apprentises or Littletonians. If thus done it may please you, as I wish it may and I hope it shall, and I with you shall be pleased: though not, yet still I am.'

We learn, from this remark, of what great importance the Essais must have been considered in literary circles, and it is not improbable that a few attempts 'of the seven or eight of great wit and worth' may have appeared in print long before Florio's translation. We may well ask: Is it likely that the greatest literary genius of his age should have been unaware of the existence of a work which was considered of such importance that 'seven or eight of great wit and worth' thought it worth while to attempt to translate it? Shakspere, who in King Henry the Fifth (1599) wrote some scenes in French, must surely have had sufficient knowledge of this language to read it.

37: Besides the quartos of 1603 and 1604, thee were reprints of the latter in 1605 and 1611; also another edition without date.

IV.
HAMLET.

In the foregoing sketch of Montaigne our especial object was to point out the inconsistency of the French writer in advising us to follow Nature as our guide, yet at the same time maintaining a strict adherence to tenets and dogmas which qualify the impulses and inclinations of nature as sinful, and which even declare war against them.

Let us see how Shakspere incarnates these contrasts in the character of Hamlet.

He makes the Danish Prince come back from the University of Wittenberg. There, we certainly may assume, he has become imbued with the new spirit that then shook the world. We refrain from mentioning it by name, because the designation we now confer upon it has become a lifeless word, comprising no longer those free thoughts of the Humanist, for which Shakspere, in this powerful tragedy, boldly enters the lists.

Hamlet longs to be back to Wittenberg. This desire represents his inclination towards free, humanistic studies. On the other hand, his adherence to old dogmatic views can be deduced from the fact of his being so terribly impressed by the circumstance of his father having had to die

   Unhousel'd, disappointed, unaneled;

a fact recorded with a threefold outcry:--

Oh, horrible! Oh, horrible! most horrible!

Again, we must direct the reader's attention to this very noteworthy point, that the first quarto edition of 'Hamlet' was already worked out tolerably well as far as the middle of the second act. For the completion of this part, only a few details were necessary. From them, we must all the more be enabled to gather Shakspere's intention.

In the speech of the Ghost in the second quarto--otherwise of well-nigh identical contents with the one in the first edition--there is only one new line, but one which deserves the closest consideration. It is that which we have quoted--

Unhousel'd, disappointed, unaneled.

The effect this statement has on the course of the dramatic action we shall explain later on. In act iii. sc. 3, where Hamlet's energy is paralysed by this disclosure of the Ghost, we afterwards again come upon a short innovation, and a most characteristic one, though but consisting of two lines.

In the first quarto we see Hamlet, in the beginning of the play, seized with an unmanly grief which makes him wish that heaven and earth would change back into chaos. But a new addition to this weariness of life is the contempt of all earthly aspirations: the aversion to Nature as the begetter of sin. The following passages are not to be found in the first quarto:--

Or that the Everlasting had not fix'd
His canon 'gainst self-slaughter! O God! God!
How weary, stale, flat, and unprofitable

Seem to me all the uses of this world!
Fie on't! Ah fie! 't is an unweeded garden,
That grows to seed; things rank and gross in nature
Possess it merely.

The scene between Hamlet and Horatio (act i. sc. 4), which in both texts is about the same, contains an innovation in which the Prince's mistrust of nature is even more sharply expressed. These lines are new:--

This heavy-headed revel east and west
Makes us traduced and tax'd of other nations--

as far as--

... The dram of eale (evil)
Doth (drawth) all the substance of a doubt
To his own scandal.

The contents of this interpolated speech may concisely be thus given: that the virtues of man, however pure and numerous they may be, are often infected by 'some vicious mole of Nature,' wherein he himself is guiltless; and that from such a fault in the chance of birth a stamp of defect is impressed upon his character, and thus contaminates the whole.

These innovations are evidently introduced for the purpose of making us understand why Hamlet does not trust to the excitements of his own reason and his own blood, in order to find out by natural means whether it be true what his 'prophetic soul' anticipates--namely, that his uncle may 'smile and smile, and yet be a villain.'

Man, says Montaigne, has no hold-fast, no firm and fixed point, within himself, in spite of his apparently splendid outfit. [1]

Man can do nothing with his own weapons alone without help from outside. In the Essay 'On the Folly of Referring the True and the False to the Trustworthiness of our Judgment,' [2] he maintains that 'it is a silly presumption to go about despising and condemning as false that which does not seem probable to us; which is a common fault of those who think they have more self-sufficiency than the vulgar. So was I formerly minded; and if I heard anybody speak either of ghosts coming back, or of the prophecy of coming things, of spells, of witchcraft, or of any other tale I could not digest--

Somnia, terrores magicos, miracula, sagas,
Nocturnos lemures, portentaque Thessala--

I felt a kind of compassion for the poor people who were made the victims of such follies. And now I find that I was, at least, to be as much pitied myself.... Reason has taught me that, so resolutely to condemn a thing as false and impossible, is to boldly assume that we have in our head the bounds and limits of the will of God and of our common mother, Nature; and I now see that there is no more notable folly in the world than to reduce them to the measure of our capacity and of our self-sufficient judgment.' [3]

Not less weak than Montaigne's trust in human reason is that of Hamlet when he fears 'the pales and forts of reason' may be broken down--

by the o'ergrowth of some complexion.

With such a mode of thought it is not to be wondered at that he should welcome the first occasion when the task of his life may be revealed to him by a heavenly messenger. Hoping that 'the questionable shape' would not let him 'burst in ignorance,' but tell him why 'we fools of Nature so horridly shake our disposition with thoughts beyond the reaches of our souls,' he follows the spectral apparition. Good Horatio does his best to restrain his friend, who has waxed 'desperate with imagination,' from approaching the 'removed ground,' that might deprive him of the 'sovereignty of reason,' and whither the Ghost beckons him.

Here there are several new lines:--

> Or to the dreadful summit of the cliff....
> The very place puts toys of desperation,
> Without more motive, into every brain
> That looks so many fathoms to the sea,
> And hears it roar beneath.

Here we have one of those incipient ecstasies of which Montaigne says that 'such transcending humours affright me as much as steep, high, and inaccessible places.' [4]

In the following scene between Hamlet and the Ghost the introduction is new:--

> Ghost. My hour is almost come,
> When I to sulphurous and tormenting flames
> Must render up myself.
> Hamlet. Alas, poor ghost!
> Ghost. Pity me not, but lend thy serious hearing
> To what I shall unfold.
> Hamlet. Speak; I am bound to hear.
> Ghost. So art thou to revenge, when thou shall hear.

This picturing of the torments of hell--how very characteristic! It is forbidden to the Ghost to communicate to 'ears of flesh and blood' the secrets of its fiery prison-house. Yet it knows how to tell enough of the horrors of that gruesome place to make the hair of a stronger mortal than Hamlet is, stand on end, 'like quills upon the fretful porcupine.'

With masterly hand, the poet depicts the distance which henceforth separates Hamlet's course of thought from that of his friends who have remained on the firm ground of human reason. Hamlet cannot say more than--

> that there's ne'er a villain dwelling in all Denmark
> But he's an arrant knave.

When Horatio answers that 'there needs no ghost, my lord, come from the grave to tell us this,' [5] Hamlet asks his friends to shake hands with him and part, giving them to understand that every man has his own business and desire, and that--

> for my own poor part,
> Look you, I'll go pray.

Horatio calls this 'wild and whirling words.' The Prince who at this moment, no doubt, expresses his own true inclination, says:--'I am sorry they offend you--heartily; yes, 'faith, heartily.' It is difficult for him to justify his own procedure. He feels unable to explain his thoughts and sentiments to the clear, unwarped reason of a Horatio, to whom the Ghost did not reply, and to whom no ghost would.

Hamlet assures his friend, for whose sympathy he greatly cares, that the apparition is a true one, an honest ghost. He advises Horatio to give the 'wondrous strange' a welcome even as to 'a stranger;' and, lest he might endeavour to test the apparition by human reason, he speaks the beautiful words:--

> There are more things in heaven and earth, Horatio,

Than are dreamt of in your philosophy

Hamlet tells his friends that in future he will put on 'an antic disposition.' Towards them he has, in fact, already done so. His desire for a threefold oath; his repeated shifting of ground; his swearing by the sword on which the hands are laid (a custom referable to the time of the Crusades, and considered tantamount to swearing by the cross, but which, at the same time, is an older Germanic, and hence Danish, custom); his use of a Latin formula, Hic et ubique--all these procedures have the evident object of throwing his comrades into a mystic frame of mind, and to make them keep silence ('so help you mercy!') as to what they have seen. These are the mysterious means which those have to use that would make themselves the medium of a message supernaturally revealed. [5]

A perusal of the fifty-sixth chapter of the first Essay of Montaigne will show with what great reverence he treated ceremonial customs and hollow formulas; for instance, the sign of the cross, of which he 'continually made use, even if he be but yawning' (sic). It is not a mere coincidence, but a well-calculated trait in the character of Hamlet, that in his speech he goes through a scale of exclamations and asseverations such as Shakspere employs in no other of his poetical creations. Hamlet incessantly mentions God, Heaven, Hell, and the Devil, the Heavenly Hosts, and the Saints. He claims protection from the latter at the appearance of the Ghost. He swears 'by St. Patrick,' by his faith, by God's wounds, by His blood, by His body, by the Cross, and so forth. [6]

Stubbs, in his 'Anatomy of Abuses' (1583), [7] lays stress, among other characteristics of the Papists, upon their terrible inclination to swearing: 'in so muche, as if they speake but three or fower words, yet must thei needes be interlaced with a bloudie othe or two, to the great dishonour of God and offence of the hearers.'

An overwhelming grief and mistrust in his own nature filled Hamlet's bold imagination with the desire of receiving a complete mandate for his mission from the hands of superior powers. So he enters the realm of mysticism, where mind wields no authority, and where no sound fruit of human reason can ripen.

Between the first and the second act there is an interval of a few months. The poet gives us no other clue to the condition and the doings of his hero than that, in the words of Polonius, [8] he 'fell into sadness; then into a fast; thence to a watch; thence into a weakness,' and so forth. We may therefore assume that he has followed his inclination to go to pray; that he tries by fasting, watching, and chastising, as so many before him, to find his way in the dreamland which he has entered following the Ghost; sincerely striving to remain true to his resolution to 'wipe from the table of his memory all pressures past.'

A new passage in the monologue of Hamlet, after the Ghost has left him, is this:--

> And thy commandment all alone shall live
> Within the book and volume of my brain,
> Unmix'd with baser matter; yes, by Heaven!
> O most pernicious woman!

We next hear about the Prince from Ophelia after the interval which, as mentioned above, lies between the first and the second act. [9] In the old play she relates that, when 'walking in the gallery all alone,' he, the lover, came towards her, altogether 'bereft of his wits.' In the scene of the later play he comes to her closet with a purpose, appearing before her in a state of mental struggle. No doubt, he then approaches her with the intention, which afterwards he carries out, of renouncing woman, the begetter of all evil in the world, which makes such monsters of wise men. The sight of his true love has shaken him. He stands before her: [10]

> ... with a look so piteous in purport
> As if he had been loosed out of hell
> To speak of horrors...
> And thrice his head thus waving up and down,
> He raised a sigh so piteous and profound
> As it did seem to shatter all his bulk
> And end his being.

Thus he leaves her, not daring to speak the word which is to separate him from her.

In the following scene between Hamlet and Polonius (act ii. sc. 2 [11]) there is again a new passage which equally proves that Hamlet's thoughts only dwell upon one theme; that is, the sinfulness of our human nature:--

> Hamlet. For if the sun breed maggots in a dead dog, being a
> god, kissing carrion--Have you a daughter?
> Polonius. I have, my lord.
> Hamlet. Let her not walk i' the sun. Conception is a blessing;
> but not as your daughter may conceive:--friend, look to't.

Hamlet said before, that 'To be honest, is to be one man picked out of ten thousand.' There is method in Hamlet's madness. With correct logic he draws from dogmas which pronounce Nature to be sinful, the conclusion that we need not wonder at the abounding of evil in this world, seeing that a God himself assists in creating it. He, therefore, warns Polonius against his daughter, too, becoming 'a breeder of sinners.'

Before we follow Hamlet now to the scene with Ophelia, where, 'in an ecstasy of divine inspiration, equally weak in reason, and violent in persuasion and dissuasion,' [12] he calls upon her to go to a nunnery, we must direct attention to the concluding part of an Essay [13] of Montaigne. It is only surprising that nobody should as yet have pointed out how unmistakeably, in that famous scene, the inconsistencies of the whimsical French writer are scourged. In that Essay the following thought occurs, which one would gladly accept as a correct one: 'Falsely do we judge the honesty *and the* beauty of an action from its usefulness. Equally wrong it is to conclude that everyone is bound to do the same, and that it is an honest action for everybody, if it be a useful one.'

Now, Montaigne endeavours to apply this thought to the institution of marriage; and he descends, in doing so, to the following irrational argument:--'Let us select the most necessary and most useful institution of human society: it is marriage. Yet the counsel of the saints deems the contrary side to be more honest; thus excluding the most venerable vocation of men.'

The satire of that famous scene in 'Hamlet' is here apparent. It will now be understood why the Danish Prince comes with a warning to his beloved, 'not to admit honesty *in discourse with* beauty,' and why his resolution is that 'we will have no more marriage.' Those words of Hamlet, too, 'this was sometime a paradox, but now the time gives it proof,' are easy of explanation. It was not yet so long ago that celibacy had been abolished in England. The 'time' now confirms celibacy once more in this French book.

Most characteristic is the following passage: in this scene the only new one. It goes far to show the intention with which the poet partly re-wrought the play. I mean the words in which Hamlet confesses to Ophelia that he has deceived her. The repentant sinner says: 'You should not have believed me: for virtue cannot so inoculate our old stock but we shall relish of it.'

Can a poet who will not convert the stage into a theological Hall of Controversy, make the soul-struggle of his hero more comprehensible? Hamlet has honestly tried (we have seen with what means) to inoculate and improve the sinful 'old stock.' But how far away he still feels himself from his aim! He calls himself 'proud, revengeful, ambitious.' These are the three sins of which he must accuse himself, when listening to the voice of Nature which admonishes him to fulfil the duty of his life--the deed of blood--that inner voice of his nobler nature which impels him to seize the crown in order to guide the destinies of his country; given over, as the latter is, to the mischievous whims of a villain.

Yet he cries out against Ophelia, 'We are arrant knaves all; believe none of us!' He reproaches this daughter of Eve with her own weaknesses and the great number of her sins in words reminding us of Isaiah, [14] where the wantonness of the daughters of Zion is reproved. He, the ascetic, calls out to his mistress: 'Go thy ways to a nunnery!... Why wouldst thou be a breeder of sinners?'

Let us hear what his mistress says about him. This passage also, explaining Hamlet's madness, is new:--

> Now see that noble and most sovereign reason,
> Like sweet bells jangled, out of tune and harsh;
> That unmatched form and feature of blown youth,
> Blasted with ecstasy. [15]

With what other word can Hamlet's passionate utterances be designated than that of religious ecstasy?

From the first moment when he sees Ophelia, and prays her to remember his sins in her 'orisons,' down to the last moment when he leaves her,

bidding her to go to a nunnery, there is method in his madness--the
method of those dogmas which brand nature and humanity as sinful,
whose impulses they do not endeavour to lead to higher aims, but which,
by certain mysteries and formulas, they pretend to be able to overcome.
The soul-struggle of Hamlet arises from his divided mind; an inner
voice of Nature calling, on the one hand:--

Let not the royal bed of Denmark be
A couch for luxury and damned incest;

whilst another voice calls out that, howsoever he pursues his act, he
should not 'taint his mind.'

In the English translation of the 'Hystorie of Hamblet,' from which
Shakspere took his subject, the art of dissembling is extolled, in
most naive language, as one specially useful towards great personages
not easily accessible to revenge. He who would exercise the arts of
dissembling (it is said there) must be able to 'kisse his hand whome
in hearte hee could wishe an hundredfoot depth under the earth, so hee
mighte never see him more, if it were not a thing wholly to bee
disliked in a Christian, who by no meanes ought to have a bitter
gall, or desires infected with revenge.'

We shall find later on that Hamlet's gall also claims its rights; all
the more so as he endeavours, by an unnatural and superstitious use of
dogmatism, to suppress and to drive away the 'excitements of the reason
and of the blood.' We have heard from Polonius that the Prince,
after his 'sadness,' fell into a 'fast.' And everything he says to
his schoolfellows Rosencrantz and Guildenstern [16] about his frame of
mind, confirms us in the belief that he has remained faithful to the
intention declared in the first act--'Look you, I will go pray'--so
as to prepare himself, like many others, to contemplate passively
a world sinful from its very nature, and therefore not to be changed

and bettered.

This scene is, in the first quarto, a mere hasty sketch, but faintly indicated. In the second quarto it is, so to say, a new one; and a comparison between the two need, therefore, not be instituted.

Before his friends Rosencrantz and Guildenstern, Hamlet, for a few moments, gives up his brain-racking thoughts of penitence; he even endeavours to philosophise, as he may have done at the University of Wittenberg before he allowed himself to be lured into dreamland. He utters a thought--'There is nothing either good or bad, but thinking makes it so'--which occurs in an Essay of Montaigne, and is thus given by Florio (127):--

'If that what we call evil and torment be neither torment nor evil, but that our fancy only gives it that quality, is it in us to change it?' [17]

Hamlet then pictures his mental condition in words of deepest sincerity. In order to fully understand this description, we have once more to refer to an Essay of Montaigne, [18] in which he asserts that man is not furthered by his reason, his speculations, his passions; that they give him no advantage over other creatures. A divinely appointed authority--the Church--confers upon him 'those great advantages and odds he supposes to have over other creatures.' It is she that seals to him the patent and privilege which authorises him to 'keep account both of the receipts and layings-out of the world.' Ay, it is she who convinces him that 'this admirable swinging-round of the heavenly vaults, the eternal light of those constellations rolling so nobly over our heads, the terrible commotions of this infinite ocean, were established, and have continued for so many ages, for his advantage and his service.' To her authority he must wholly surrender himself; by her he must allow himself to be guided. And in doing so, it is 'better for us to have a weak judgment than a strong one; better to be smitten with blindness than to have one's eyes open and clear-sighted.'

Striving to live up to similar views, Hamlet 'lost all his mirth.' This is the cause of his heavy disposition; of his having 'foregone all custom of exercise'--so 'that this goodly frame, the earth,' seems to him 'a sterile promontory,' a mere place of preparation for gaining the next world through penance and prayer. Verily, 'this brave o'erhanging firmament, this majestical roof fretted with golden fire,' appears to him no better 'than a foul and pestilent congregation of vapours.' Quite in accordance with such tenets which we need not qualify by name, Man, to him, is but a 'quintessence of dust.'

Both man, and still more sinful woman, displease Hamlet. Yet he has not succeeded in so wholly subjugating Nature within himself as to be fully secured against her importunate claims. Now we would point out here that Montaigne [19] mentions a tyrant of antiquity who 'could not bear seeing tragedies acted in the theatre, from fear that his subjects should see him sob at the misfortunes of Hecuba and Andromache--him who, without pity, caused daily so many people to be cruelly killed.' Again, Montaigne [20] speaks of actors, mentioned by Quinctilian, who were 'so deeply engaged in a sorrowful part that they wept even after having returned to their lodgings;' whilst Quinctilian reports of himself that, 'having undertaken to move a certain passion in others, he had entered so far into his part as to find himself surprised, not only with the shedding of tears, but also with a paleness of countenance and the behaviour of a man truly weighed down with grief.'

Hamlet has listened to the player. In the concluding monologue of the second act--which is twice as long in the new quarto--we are told of the effect produced upon his mind when seeing that an actor, who merely holds a mirror up to Nature--

> ... but in a fiction, in a dream of passion,
> Could force his soul so to his own conceit
> That from her working all his visage wann'd....
> ... And all for nothing!--For Hecuba?

whilst he (Hamlet), 'a dull and muddy-mettled rascal,' [21] like John-a-dreams, in spite of his strong 'motive and the cue for passion,' mistrusts them and is afraid of being guided by them.

All at once, Hamlet feels the weight and pressure of a mode of thought which declares war against the impulses of Nature, calling man a born sinner.

> Who calls me villain? ...
> ... Gives me the lie i' the throat,
> As deep as to the lungs? Who does me this?
> Ha!
> 'S wounds,[1] I should take it: for it cannot be.
> But I am pigeon-liver'd, and lack gall
> To make oppression bitter; or ere this
> I should have fatted all the region kites
> With this slave's offal. [22]

The feelings of Hamlet, until then forcibly kept down, now get the mastery over him. He gives vent to them in oaths of which he is himself at last ashamed, when he compares himself to 'a very drab, a scullion,' who 'must fall a-cursing.'

He now will set to work and get more natural evidence of the King's guilt. He begins to entertain doubts as to those mystic views by which he meant to be guided. He mistrusts the apparition which he had called an honest ghost ('true-penny'):--

> The spirit that I have seen
> May be the Devil: and the Devil hath power
> To assume a pleasing shape. Yea, perhaps
> Out of my weakness and my melancholy,
> As he is very potent with such spirits,
> Abuses me to damn me: I'll have grounds
> More relative than this. [23]

Over weakness the Devil is potent; all flesh is weak. What mode of thought is this? What philosophy taught this doctrine? Hamlet's weakness, if we may believe Polonius, [24] has been brought on by fasting and watching.

Over melancholy, too, the Devil is powerful. Are we not here in the sombre atmosphere of those who turn away their reason from ideal aspirations; who denounce the impulses of nature as sinful excitements; who would fain look upon the earth as 'a sterile promontory'--having dark death more before their mind's eye than beautiful life? Are such thoughts not the forerunners of melancholy?

Hamlet's incessant thoughts of death are the same as those of his model, Montaigne. In an Essay, [25] entitled 'That to Philosophise is to Learn how to Die,' the latter explains that the Christian religion has no surer basis than the contempt for the present life, and that we are in this world only to prepare ourselves for death. His imagination, he says, has occupied itself with these thoughts of death more than with anything else. Referring to a saying of Lykurgos, he approves of graveyards being laid out close to churches and in the most frequented places of a city, so as to accustom the common people, women, and children not to be scared at the sight of a dead person, and to forewarn everyone, by this continual spectacle of bones, tombs, and funerals, as to our real condition.

Montaigne also, like Hamlet, ponders over suicide. He devotes a whole
Essay [26] to it. Life, he observes, would be a tyranny if the liberty
to die were wanting. For this liberty, he thinks, we have to thank
Nature, as for the most favourable gift which, indeed, deprives us
of all right to complain of our condition. If--as Boiocal, the German
chieftain, [27] said--earth is wanting to us whereon to live, earth
is never wanting to us for death. [28]

That is the wisdom of Montaigne, the admirer of antiquity. But
Montaigne, the modern man, introduces the Essay in which he dares to
utter such bold thoughts with the following restriction:--

'If, as it is said, to philosophise be to doubt, with much more reason
to play pranks (niaiser) and to rave, as I do, must be to doubt.
For, to inquire and to discuss, behoves the disciples. The decision
belongs to the chairman (cathedrant). My chairman is the
authority of the divine will which regulates us without contradiction,
and which occupies its rank above those human and vain disputes.'
This chairman, as often observed, by which Montaigne's thoughts are
to be guided, is an ecclesiastic authority.

In 'Hamlet,' also, it is a 'canon' [29] fixed against self-slaughter,
which restrains him from leaving, out of his own impulse, this whilom
paradise, this 'unweeded garden' of life.

Montaigne, whose philosophy aims at making us conversant with death
as with a friend, is yet terrified by it. Altogether, he says, he would
fain pass his life at his ease; and if he could escape from blows,
even by taking refuge under a calf's skin, [30] he would not be the
man who would shrink from it.

In a few graphic words Shakspere brands this cowardly clinging to life.
In the scene where Hamlet gives to Polonius nothing more willingly

than his leave, the new quarto (in every other respect the conclusion of this scene is identical in both editions) contains these additional words:--'Except my life, except my life, except my life.' Of the 'calf's skin' we hear in the first scene of act v., where those are called sheep and calves, who seek out assurance in parchments which are made of sheep-skins and of calves-skins too.

Montaigne, who does not cease pondering over the pale fellow, Death, looks for consolation from the ancients. He takes Sokrates as the model of all great qualities; and he reproduces, in his own manner, the speech this sage, who was fearless of death, made before his judges. First of all, he makes him say that the qualities of death are unknown to him, as he has never seen anybody who could instruct him in them. 'Those who fear death, presuppose that they know it.... Perhaps death may be an indifferent thing; perhaps a desirable one. However, one may believe that, if it be a transmigration from one place to another, it will be an amelioration ... and free us from having any more to do with wicked and corrupt judges. If it be a consummation (aneantissement) [31] of our being, it is also an amelioration to enter into a long and quiet night. We find nothing so sweet in life as a quiet rest--a tranquil and profound sleep without dreams.'

Now compare the monologue, 'To be or not to be,' of the first quarto with the one contained in the second. It will then be seen that those Sokratic ideas, rendered by Montaigne in his own manner, have been worked into the first quarto. In the latter we hear nothing at all about the end of our being (a complete destruction or consummation) producing an amelioration. [32] Shakspere expresses this thought by the words that if we could say that, by a sleep, we 'end the heartache and the thousand natural shocks that flesh is heir to--'tis a consummation devoutly to be wished.' [33]

Keen commentators have pointed out the contradiction in Hamlet's monologue, where he speaks of--

> The undiscovered country from whose bourn
> No traveller returns,

whilst he saw such a traveller in his father's ghost. Certainly there were then, even as there are now, besides the logical thinkers, also a considerable number of inconsistent persons who believed in supernaturally revealed messages, and who, nevertheless, now and then, felt contradictory thoughts rising within themselves. Why should the great master, who exhausted in his dramatic personages almost all types of human nature, not have put such a character also on the stage?

To the poet, whose object it was to show 'to the very age and body of time his form and pressure' (this passage is wanting in the first quarto), the presentation of such a psychological problem of contradictory thoughts must have been of far greater attraction than an anticipatory description of a metaphysician aching under the heavy burden of his philosophic speculations. The latter is the character attributed, by some, to Hamlet. But we think that such an utterly strange modern creature would have been altogether incomprehensible to the energetic English mind of this period.

In the course of the drama, Shakspere makes it sufficiently clear that the thoughts by which Hamlet's 'native hue of resolution is sicklied o'er,' have come from the narrow cells of a superstitious Christianity, not from the free use of his reason. According to Montaigne, however, we ought to 'use our reason only for strengthening our belief.'

Hamlet, with Purgatory and Hell, into which he has cast a glance, before his eyes, would fain fly, like Montaigne, from them. In his Essay I. 19 [34] the latter says that our soul must be steeled against the powers of death; 'for, as long as Death frightens us, how is it possible to make a single step without feverish agitation?'

Hamlet as little attains this condition of quiet equanimity as the pensive and pondering Montaigne. The latter, however, speaks of souls that know no fear. It is true, he has to go to the ancients in order to meet with this frame of mind. Quoting Horace [35]--

Non vultus instantis tyranni
Mente quatit solida, neque Auster,
Dux inquieti turbidus Adriae,
Nec fulminantis magna Jovis manus--

he describes such a soul as being made 'mistress over her passions and concupiscence; having become proof against poverty and disgrace, and all the other injuries of fortune. Let those who can, gain this advantage. Herein lies true and sovereign freedom that allows us to scorn force and injustice, and to deride prisons and fetters.'

To a friend with such a soul, to a living Horace or Horatio, Hamlet addresses himself. Horatio also is his fellow-student and friend from the University days at Wittenberg, and he has made the views of the new philosophical school quite his own. He does not tremble before the fire of Purgatory and Hell. Despising death, he wishes, in the last scene, to empty the cup of poison from which his friend Hamlet has drunk, in order to follow him. When the latter keeps him back, Horatio makes answer--

I am more an antique Roman than a Dane.

Hamlet, trusting more to this firmer and truly antique character than to his own, requests Horatio to aid him during the play-scene in watching the King, so as to procure more natural evidence of his guilt.

This school-friend--how often may he have philosophised with him!--is to him

> as just a man
> As e'er my conversation coped withal.

The following passage, [36] in which Horatio's character is described by Hamlet, is wanting in the first quarto:--

> Since my dear soul was mistress of her choice,
> And could of men distinguish, her election
> Hath seal'd thee for herself; for thou hast been
> As one, in suffering all, that suffers nothing;
> A man that fortune's buffets and rewards
> Hath ta'en with equal thanks: and blest are those
> Whose blood and judgment are so well commingled
> That they are not a pipe for Fortune's finger
> To sound what stop she please. Give me that man
> That is not passion's slave, and I will wear him
> In my heart's core, ay, in my heart of heart,
> As I do thee.

How near these words of Shakspere come to those with which Montaigne describes an intrepid man after the poem of Horace!

But, in spite of subtle reasoning, the French philosopher cannot fathom the cause why he himself does not attain any mind's ease, and why he has no plain and straightforward faculty (nulle faculte simple) within himself. He once [37] uses the expression, 'We trouble death with the care of life, and life with the care of death;' but he does not succeed in firmly attaching himself to life with all the fibres of his nature, and gathering strength from the mother-earth, like Antaeus. He oscillates between two antagonistic views, and feels unable to decide for either the one or the other.

We have explained the elements of which Hamlet's complex character is made up. He is an adherent of old superstitions and dogmas; he believes in Purgatory, a Hell, and a Devil, and in the miraculous powers of confession, holy communion, and the extreme unction. Yet, to some degree, he is a Humanist, and would fain grant to Nature certain rights. Scarcely has he yielded to the impulses of his blood, than doubts begin to rise in him, and he begins to fear the Devil, who might lure him into perdition. This inner discord, creating, as it does, a mistrust in his own self, induces him, in the most important task of his life, to appeal to Horatio. To him he says that, if the King's occulted guilt does not come out ('unkennel itself'), he (Hamlet) will look upon the apparition as a damned ghost, and (this is new) will think that his 'imaginations are as foul as Vulcan's stithy.' [38]

By the interlude, Hamlet--and in this he is confirmed by Horatio--becomes convinced of the King's guilt. All that he thereupon does is--to recite a little ditty!

We have already made the acquaintance of Montaigne the soft-hearted, who, as above mentioned, always was touched when seeing innocent animals hunted to death, and who felt much emotion at the tears of the hart asking us for mercy. At the same time we have directed the reader's attention to the fact of his having said that the 'common weal requires some to betray, some to lie, and some to massacre,' [39] and that this task must be left to those who are ready to sacrifice their honour and their conscience, and that men who do not feel up to such deeds must leave their commission to the stronger ones. This French nobleman naively avows that he has resolved upon withdrawing into private life, not because he is averse to public life--for the latter, he says, would 'perhaps equally suit him'--but because, by doing so, he hopes to serve his Prince all the

more joyfully and all the more sincerely, thus following the free
choice of his own judgment and reason, and not submitting to any
restraint (obligation particuliere), which he hates in every
shape. And he adds the following curious moral doctrine:--'This is
the way of the world. We let the laws and precepts follow their way,
but we keep another course.' [40]

Who could mistake Shakspere's satire against this sentimental nobleman,
who fights shy of action, in making Hamlet recite a little ditty at a
moment when he has become convinced of the King's guilt:--

> Why, let the stricken deer go weep,
> The hart ungalled play;
> For some must watch, while some must sleep:
> Thus runs the world away.

This gifted Frenchman, Montaigne, was a new, a strange, phenomenon
in the eyes of Shakspere and his active and energetic countrymen.
A man, a nobleman too, who lives for no higher aim; who allows himself
to be driven about, rudderless, by his feelings and inclinations;
who even boasts of this mental disposition of his, and sends a vain
book about it into the world! What is it to teach? What good is it
to do? It gives mere words, behind which there is no manly character.
Are there yet more beaux esprits to arise who, in Epicurean
fashion, enjoy the beautiful thoughts of others, whilst they themselves
remain incapable for action, letting the time go out of joint?

Let us further study the character of Hamlet, and we shall find that
the satire against Montaigne becomes more and more striking--a veritable
hit.

The Queen asks for her son. Before he fulfils her wish and comes to her,
he utters a lullaby of superstition (these lines are new), wherewith to

tide over the excitement of his nature:--

> 'Tis now the very witching time of night,
> When churchyards yawn and hell itself breathes out
> Contagion to this world: now could I drink hot blood,
> And do such bitter business as the day
> Would quake to look on.

Hamlet, always shrinking back from the impulses of his blood, fears that the Devil might once more gain power over him:--

> Soft! now to my mother!
> O heart, lose not thy nature!

This nature of his, inclining to mildness and gentleness, he wishes to preserve, and he resolves upon being 'cruel, not unnatural.' In vain one seeks here for logic, and for the boundary between two words which to ordinary common sense appear synonymous. In Montaigne, however, we discover the clue of such a senseless argumentation. In one of his Essays, [41] which contains a confusion of ideas that might well make the humane Shakspere shudder, he writes:--

'Our condition, both public and private, is full of imperfections; yet there is nothing useless in Nature, not even uselessness itself.... Our being is cemented with sickly qualities: ambition, jealousy, envy, vengeance, superstition, despair dwell in us, and hold there so natural a possession that their counterfeit is also recognised in beasts; for instance, cruelty--so unnatural a vice. Yet he who would root out the seed of these qualities from the human breast would destroy the fundamental conditions of our life.'

Now, Hamlet's resolution to be 'cruel, but not unnatural,' is but a fresh satire against Montaigne's train of thoughts, who would fain be a Humanist, but who does not break with the reasoning of Loyola and of the Church, by which he permits himself to be guided as by the competent authority, and which tolerates cruelty--nay, orders its being employed for the furtherance of what it calls the 'good aim.'

The idea that cruelty is a necessary but useful evil, no doubt induced Montaigne [42] to declare that to kill a man from a feeling of revenge is tantamount to our protecting him, for we thus 'withdraw him from our attacks.' Furthermore, this Humanist argues that revenge is to be regretted if its object does not feel its intention; for, even as he who takes revenge intends to derive pleasure from it, so he upon whom revenge is taken must perceive that intention, in order to be harrowed with feelings of pain and repentance. 'To kill him, is to render further attacks against him impossible; not to revenge what he has done.'

Shakspere already gives Hamlet an opportunity in the following scene to prove to us that there is no boundary between cruel and unnatural conduct; and that one cannot be cruel and yet remain natural. In the most telling words, the cause of Hamlet's want of energy is substantiated. Fate gives the criminal, the King, into the hands of Hamlet. It is the most important moment of the drama. A stroke of the sword would be enough to do the deed of revenge. The cause which makes Hamlet hesitate is, that the criminal is engaged in prayer, and that--

> He took my father grossly, full of bread,
> With all his crimes broad-blown, as flush as May;
> And how his audit stands, who knows save Heaven?

Does Hamlet, then, not act with refined cruelty?

Here, a new thought is inserted, which we mentioned already in the beginning, and which turns the balance at the decisive moment:--

> But in our circumstance and course of thought
> It is heavy with him. [43]

A Shaksperean hero, with drawn sword, allows himself to be restrained from action by the thought that, because 'it is heavy' with his own murdered father, who is suffering in Purgatory, he (Hamlet) ought not to kill the criminal now, but later on, when the latter is deeply wading in sin--

> When he is drunk asleep, or in his rage, ...
> And that his soul may be as damn'd and black
> As Hell, whereto it goes.

Hamlet has been called a philosopher whose energy has been paralysed by too great a range of thought. For the sovereignty of human reason this is a most dangerous premiss. Do we not owe to the full and free use of that reason everything great which mankind has created? History speaks of a thousand heroes (only think of Alexander, of Julius Caesar, of Frederick the Great!) whose doings convince us that a strong power of thought and action can go hand in hand, nay, that the latter cannot be successful without the former.

But, on the other hand, there is a way of thinking with preconceived supernatural conclusions--or rather, we must call it an absence of thinking--when men allow themselves to be moved by the circumstances of a traditional course of thought. Against such intellectual slavery the great century of the Reformation rose. And the greatest Humanist, Shakspere, scourges that slavery in the catharsis of his powerful drama.

Questions of religion were not permitted to be treated on the stage.

But not merely the one deeply intelligent person for whom Shakspere asks the players to act, and for whom the great master certainly endeavoured to write--no, the public at large, too, will have understood that the 'course of thought' which induced Hamlet to forego action from a subtle refinement of cruelty, was not the course of thought prevalent on this side of the Channel, and held up, in this important scene, as that of a hero to be admired.

Hamlet resolved upon keeping out the soul of Nero from his 'firm bosom.' (What a satire there is in this adjective 'firm'!) He means to be cruel, but not unnatural; he will 'speak daggers, but use none.' A man who lets himself be moved by extraneous circumstances is not his own master. In cruel, unnatural manner, for no object whatever, he murders poor Polonius. Then he begins to speak daggers in such a manner as to get into a perfect ecstasy. Nor need any priest have been ashamed of the sermon he preaches to his own mother.

In the first edition of 'Hamlet,' the scene between mother and son is rather like a sketch in which most things are merely indicated, not worked out. Only the part of the Ghost, with the exception of the line:--

  Conceit in weakest bodies strongest works,

which is wanting in the first edition, and Hamlet's address to the Ghost, are in both quartos the same. Even as in the first act, so this time also, Hamlet, on seeing the Ghost, calls upon the saints:--

  Save me, and hover o'er me with your wings,
    You heavenly guards!

This was the usual course on the occasion of such doubtful apparitions, of which one did not know whether they were 'airs of heaven' or 'blasts from hell.'

A new intercalation is (in the first quarto there is no vestige of it), that Hamlet reproaches his mother with having degraded 'sweet religion' to 'a rhapsody of words;' that he says 'the Devil hath conquered her at hoodman blind ;' that she should confess herself to Heaven, and 'assume a virtue if she have it not;' that 'virtue itself of vice must pardon beg in the fatness of these pursy times, yea, curb and woo, for leave to do him good.' So also is the Queen's question new:--

> Ay me, what act,
> That roars so loud, and thunders in the index? [44]

There is no trace, in the first quarto, of the following most characteristic thoughts:--

> For, use almost can change the stamp of Nature [45]
> And either curb (?) the Devil, or throw him out
> With wondrous potency....
> And when you are desirous to be blest,
> I'll blessing beg of you.

Let us figure to ourselves before what public Hamlet first saw the wanderer from Purgatory; before what youth he bade Ophelia go to a nunnery; before what men he remained inactive at the critical moment simply because the criminal is engaged in his prayers, whilst his own murdered father died without Holy Communion, without having confessed and received the Extreme Unction. Let us remember before what audience he purposely made the thunders of the Index roar so loud; at what place he gets into ecstasy; and where he first preaches to his mother that the Devil may be mastered and thrown out.

Here, certainly, we have questions of religion!

Shakspere's genius has known how to transport these most important questions of his time, away from the shrill contact with contemporary disputes, into the harmonious domain of the Muses. He, and his friends and patrons, did not look upon the subjects discussed in this tragedy with the passionless, indifferent eyes of our century. Many men, no doubt, were filled with the thought, to which Bacon soon gave a scientific form, that the human mind can only make true progress if it turns towards the inquiry into Nature, keeping far away from the hampering influence of transcendental dogmas. The liberal, intellectual tendencies of the Reformation were not yet fettered in England with the new dogmatic strait waistcoat of a narrow-minded, melancholy sect. And Shakspere's views, which he has embodied in 'Hamlet,' were not in divinatory advance of his age; they were easily comprehensible to the best of his time.

Our chief argument will be contained in the chapter in which we shall hear Shakspere's adversaries launch out furiously against the tendency of this drama. Meanwhile, we will exhaust the course of its action.

Hamlet has already come very near to that point of view where Reason at last ceases to guide his conduct, and where he becomes convinced that indiscretion often is of better service than deep planning.

Now in Montaigne's Essay [46] already mentioned we read:--'When an urgent circumstance, or any violent or unexpected accident of State necessity, induces a Prince to break his word and faith, or otherwise forces him out of his ordinary duty, he is to ascribe that compulsion to a lash of God's rod.'

The passage in which Hamlet consoles himself in regard to the murder committed against Polonius is new:--

  I do repent: but heaven hath pleased it so,

To punish me with this, and this with me,
That I must be their scourge and minister.

Hamlet, beholding the victim of his indiscretion, excuses himself thus:--

I must be cruel, only to be kind.

The cruel deed he has done, he palliates with the remark that lovingkindness has forced him to it. Love of her God also forced Catherine of Medicis to the massacre of St. Bartholomew.

Thus bad begins, and worse remains behind.

Yes; worse is coming! Hamlet knows that he is to be sent to England; that the letters are sealed; that his two schoolfellows whom he trusts as he will adders, bear the mandate. What does he do to prevent further misfortune?

He rejoices that--

they must sweep my way,
And marshall me to knavery. [47]

He enjoys, in advance, the sweet presentiment of revenge which he intends taking upon them. He lets things go without hindrance:--

Let it work!
For 'tis sport to have the engineer
Hoist with his own petard.

He enjoys his own crafty policy which shall blow his school-friends, Rosencrantz and Guildenstern (who yet, so far as he knows, have not been guilty in any way towards him!) 'at the moon:'--

> O, 'tis most sweet
> When in one line two crafts directly meet.

Because Hamlet gives utterance to high-sounding thoughts, to sentimental dreams, and melancholy subtleties, it has been assumed that his character is one nourished with the poet's own heart's blood. A thousand times the noble sentiment of duty has been dwelt upon, which it is alleged he is inspired with; and on account of his fine words he has been more taken a fancy to than any other Shaksperian figure. But that was not the poet's object. Great deeds were more to him than the finest words. His contemporaries understood him; for Montaigne--as we shall prove--was given over to the lowest scorn of the age through 'Hamlet,' because the whole reasoning of Hamlet not only was a fruitless, but a pernicious one.

In the fourth scene of the fourth act, the poet describes the frame of mind of the hero before he steps on board ship. 'Excitements of his reason and his blood' once more call him to revenge. This monologue, in which Hamlet gives expression to his feelings and thoughts, is only in the quarto of 1604. The folio of 1623 does not contain it. Shakspere, in later years, may have thought that the soul-struggle of his hero had been ended; and so he may have regarded the passage as a superfluous one, in which Hamlet's better self once more asks him to seize the reins of destiny with his own hands.

He sees how young Fortinbras, the delicate and tender prince, 'puff'd with divine ambition, mouthes the invisible event for a piece of land not large enough to hide the slain.' Hamlet philosophises that the man who uses not his god-like reason is but a beast; for--

> --He that made us with such large discourse
> Looking before and after, gave us not
> That capability and god-like reason,

To fust in us unused.

We further hear how Hamlet reasons about the question as to how 'to be rightly great.' All the thoughts he produces, seem to flow from the pen of the French philosopher. In Essay III. (13) of Montaigne we read the beautiful words that 'the noblest master-work of man is to live for a purpose (yivre d fropos),' and:--'The greatness of the soul does not consist so much in drawing upwards, and haling forwards, than in knowing how to range and to circumscribe itself. It holds everything to be great, which is sufficient in itself. It shows its superiority in more loving humble things than eminent ones.'

To the majesty of the human reason also, Montaigne, in spite of his so often condemning it, knows how to render justice. In Essay I. (40) he remarks: 'Shall we then dare to say that this advantage of reason at which we rejoice so very much, and out of respect for which we hold ourselves to be lords and emperors of all other creatures, has been put into us for our torment? Why strive for the knowledge of things if we become more cowardly thereby? if we lose, through it, the rest and the tranquillity in which we should be without it? ... Shall we use the intellect that has been given to us for our greatest good, to effect our ruin; combating the designs of Nature and the general order of things which implies that everyone should use his tools and means for his own convenience?'

Noble thoughts! But it is not enough to play an aesthetic game with them. The energetic English genius wishes that they should regulate our life; that we should act in accordance with them, so that no tragic complication should form itself, which could only be solved by the ruin and death of the innocent together with the guilty. The monologue concludes thus:--

> O, from this time forth,
> My thoughts be bloody, or be nothing worth!

Nevertheless, Hamlet continues his voyage.

The reader will remember that Montaigne spoke of an instinctive impulse of the will--a daimon--by which he often, and to his final advantage, had allowed himself to be guided, so much so that such strong impulses might be attributed to divine inspiration. A daimon of this kind, under whose influence Hamlet acts, is described in the second scene of the fifth act. The passage is wanting in the first quarto. [48] Hamlet tells Horatio how he lay in the ship, and how in his heart there was a kind of fighting which would not let him sleep. This harassing condition, the result of his unmanly indecision, he depicts in these words:--

> Methought I lay
> Worse than the mutines in the bilboes.

Then all at once (how could an impulsive manner of action be better described?), before he could 'make a prologue to his brains,' Hamlet lets himself be overcome by such a daimonic influence. He breaks open the grand commission of others, forges a seal with a signet in his possession, becomes a murderer of two innocent men, and draws the evil conclusion therefrom:--

> Let us know,
> Our indiscretion sometimes serves us well,
> When our deep plots do pall; and that should learn us,
> There's a divinity that shapes our ends,
> Rough-hew them how we will.

This view we have already quoted from Essay III. (12). In Florio's translation (632):--'Therefore do our dessigns so often miscarry....

The heavens are angry, and I may say envious of the extension
and large privilege we ascribe to human wisdome, to the prejudice of
theirs: and abridge them so more unto us, by so much more we endeavour
to amplifie them.'

Hamlet takes the twofold murder committed against Rosencrantz and
Guildenstern as little to heart as the 'indiscreet' deed by which
Polonius was killed. Then the consolation was sufficient for him that
lovingkindness had forced him to be cruel. This time, his conscience
is not touched, because--

  't is dangerous when the baser nature comes
  Between the pass and fell incensed points
  Of mighty opposites.

With such argumentation every tyranny may be palliated, especially by
those who, like Hamlet, think that--

  A man's life 's no more than to say 'One.'

Yet another peculiarity of Montaigne's complex being is depicted by
Shakspere in the graveyard scene. He shows us every side of this
whimsical character who says of himself that he has no staying power
for any standpoint, but that he is driven about by incalculable
emergencies.

Let us read a passage in Essay II (12), and compare it with Hamlet's
enigmatic conduct towards Laertes. Montaigne describes himself in
these sentences:--'Being of a soft and somewhat heavy temperament, I
have no great experience of those violent agitations which mostly
come like a surprise upon our mind without allowing it leisure to
collect itself.' In spite of the resistance--he further says--which
he endeavoured to offer, even he, however, was occasionally thus

seized. He felt these agitations rising and growing in, and becoming master over, himself. As in drunkenness, things then appeared to him otherwise than he usually saw them. 'I manifestly saw the advantages of the object which I sought after, augmenting and growing; and I felt them becoming greater and swelling by the wind of my imagination. I felt the difficulties of my enterprise becoming easier and simpler, my reasoning and my conscience drawing back. But, that fire being gone, all of a sudden, as with the flash of lightning, my mind resumed another view, another condition, another judgment.'

In this manner Hamlet conducts himself towards Laertes. A great grief takes possession of him when he hears of the death of Ophelia: he leaps, like Laertes, into her grave; he grapples with him; he warns him that, though 'not splenetive and rash,' he (Hamlet) yet has 'something dangerous' in him. (He means the daimon which so fatally impelled him against Rosencrantz and Guildenstern.) Hamlet and Laertes wrestle, but they are parted by the attendants. Hamlet begins boasting, in high-flown language, of what great things he would be able to do.

The Queen describes Hamlet's rage in these words:--

> And thus awhile the fit will work on him;
> Anon, as patient as the female dove,
> When that her golden couplets are disclosed,
> His silence will sit drooping. [49]

In the meantime, the fire with which Hamlet's soul had been seized, is gone, like a flash of lightning. He changes to another point of view--probably that one according to which everything goes its way in compliance with a heavenly decree. The little verse he recites in parting:--

Let Hercules himself do what he may,

The cat will mew and dog will have his day,

quite corresponds to such a passive philosophy which has gained the mastery over him, and to which he soon falls a victim.

We are approaching the conclusion of the great drama. Here, again, in order to explain Hamlet's action, or rather his yielding to influences around him, we have to direct the attention of the reader to Essay (III. 10), in which Montaigne tells how easily he protects himself against the dangers of inward agitation by dropping the subject which threatens to become troublesome to him before he is drawn on and carried along by it. The doughty nobleman says that he has escaped from many difficulties by not staking frivolously, like others, happiness and honour, life and everything, on his 'rapier and his dagger.' [50]

There may be some truth in Montaigne's charge that the cause of not a few struggles he has seen, was often of truly pitiful origin, and that such struggles were only carried on from a mistaken feeling of self-respect. It may be true also that it is a bad habit--as he maintains--to proceed still further in affairs of this kind simply because one is implicated. But how strange a confession of a nobleman from whom we at all times expect bravery: 'For want of judgement our hearte fails us.' [51]

Hamlet is engaged in such a struggle with Laertes through the graveyard scene. The King, who has had good cause to study Hamlet's character more deeply than anyone else, reckons upon his vanity in order to decide him to the fencing-match. 'Rapier and dagger' are forced upon weak-willed Hamlet by Osric. [52] How subtle is this satire! For appearance' sake, in order to outshine Laertes, the Prince accepts the challenge. [53] Happiness and life, which he ought long ago to have risked for the purpose of avenging his father and his honour, are now staked from sheer vanity. The 'want of prudence' Hamlet displays in accepting a challenge which he must 'carry out from a (mistaken) feeling of self-respect,' has the 'intolerable' consequence that, shortly before he crosses swords with Laertes, he confesses to Horatio:--'But thou would'st not think how ill all's here about my heart.'

Again, Shakspere, very briefly, but not less pointedly, depicts the way in which Hamlet allows himself to be influenced and driven to a decision. This time the poet does so by bringing in a clearly expressed dogmatic tenet whereby Hamlet's fate is sealed. It is 'ill all about his heart.' He would prefer not going to meet Laertes. [54]

> Horatio. If your mind dislike anything, obey it. I will forestal their repair hither, and say you are not fit.

The fatalist Hamlet, whom we have seen coming ever closer to the doctrine of Predestination, answers as follows:--

'Not a whit; we defy augury; there is special providence in the fall of a sparrow. [55] If it be now, 'tis not to come; if it be not to come, it will be now; if it be not now, yet it will come; the readiness is all. Since no man has aught of what he leaves, what is't to leave betimes? Let be.'

This time it is a 'Let be!'--even as it was a 'Let it go' when he was sent to England.

Now let us read Montaigne's Essay, [56] 'To Philosophise is to Learn how to Die:'--

'Our religion has had no surer human foundation than the contempt of life. Not only does the course of our reason lead us that way; for, why should we fear to lose a thing which, when lost, cannot be regretted?--but also, seeing that we are threatened by so many kinds of death, is it not a greater inconvenience to fear them all than to endure one? What does it matter when Death comes, since it is inevitable?... Moreover, nobody dies before his hour. The time you leave behind was no more yours than that which was before your birth, and concerns you no more.'

No further comment is needed to prove that Hamlet's and Montaigne's thoughts are in so close a connection that it cannot be a mere accident. And the nearer we come to the conclusion of the drama, the more striking become Shakspere's satirical hits.

Hamlet allows his hand to be put into that of Laertes by the King. He does not think of the wrong he has done to Laertes--of the murder of the latter's father, or the unhappiness he has criminally brought upon Laertes' sister. In most cowardly manner, hoping that Laertes would desist from the combat, Hamlet endeavours to excuse his conduct at the grave of Ophelia, by pleading his own madness. Laertes insists on the combat; adding that he would stand aloof 'till by some elder masters of known honour' the decision were given.

Hamlet avenges the death of his father; he kills the criminal, the enemy, when his wrath is up and aflame, and every muscle of his is swelled with indignation--but it is too late. Together with himself, he has dragged them all into the grave. It is blind passion, unbridled by reason, which does the deed: a sublime satire upon the words of Montaigne in Essay II. (12), 'that the most beautiful actions of the soul proceed from, and have need of, this impulse of passion; valour, they say, cannot become perfect without the help of wrath; and that nobody pursues the wicked and the enemies with sufficient energy, except he be thoroughly in anger.'

Even the kind of death by which Shakspere makes Hamlet lose his life, looks like a satire against Montaigne. The latter, always a coward in regard to death, and continually pondering over it, says: [57]--'I would rather have chosen to drink the potion of Sokrates than wound myself as Cato did.' Their 'virtuous deeds' he calls [58] 'vain and fruitless ones, because they were done from no love of, or obedience to, the true Creator of all things.'

Hamlet dies wounded and poisoned, as if Shakspere had intended expressing his abhorrence of so vacillating and weak-willed a character, who places the treacherous excesses of passion above the power of that human reason in whose free service alone Greeks and Romans did their most exalted deeds of virtue. [59]

The subtlety of the best psychologists has endeavoured to fix the limits of Hamlet's madness, and to find the proper name for it. No agreement has been arrived at. We think we have solved the problem as to the nature of Hamlet's madness, and to have shown why thought and action, in him, cannot be brought into a satisfactory harmony. Every fibre in Shakspere's artistic mind would have rebelled against the idea of making a lunatic the chief figure of his greatest drama. He wished to warn his contemporaries that the attempt of reconciling two opposite circles of ideas--namely, on the one hand, the doctrine that we are to be guided by the laws of Nature; and on the other, the yielding ourselves up to superstitious dogmas which declare human nature to be sinful--must inevitably produce deeds of madness.

The main traits of Montaigne's character Shakspere confers upon the Danish Prince, and places him before a difficult task of life. He is to avenge his father's death. (Montaigne was attached to his father with all his soul, and speaks of him almost in the same words as Hamlet does of his own.) He is to preserve the State whose legitimate sovereign he is. The materials for a satire are complete. And it is written in such a manner as to remain the noblest, the most sublime poetical production as long as men shall live.

The two circles of ideas which in the century of the Reformation began a struggle that is not yet brought to an end, are, in that drama, represented on the stage. The poet shows, by making the gifted Prince perish, on which side every serious thinker ought to place himself. That these intentions of Shakspere were understood by his more intelligent contemporaries and friends, we shall prove when we come to the camp of his adversaries, at whose head a Roman Catholic stood, who launches out in very marked language against the derision of Montaigne as contained in the character of Hamlet.

The noblemen who went to the theatre for the sake of the intellectual attractions (the fairer sex being still excluded from acting on the stage and therefore not forming a point of attraction) were initiated into the innermost secret of what authors meant by their productions. Dekker, in his 'Gulls Horn Book' (c. 6), reports that 'after the play was over, poets adjourned to supper with knights, where they, in private, unfolded the secret parts of their drama to them.'

As in no other of his plays, there is in Shakspere's 'Hamlet'--the drama richest in philosophy--a perfect wealth of life. Argument is pitted against argument; every turn of a phrase is a missile, sharp, and hitting the mark. In not a few cases, the aim and object is no longer recognisable. Here and there we believe we shall be able to shed the light of day upon some dark passages of the past.

To the doughty friends of Shakspere, this French Knight of the Order of St. Michael, who says [60] that, if his freedom were in the least encroached upon, or 'if the laws under which he lives threatened merely the tip of his finger, he would at once betake himself to any other place to find better ones;' but who yet lets everything around him go out of joint without offering a helping hand for repair, because 'the maintenance of States is probably something beyond our powers of understanding' [61]--verily, to Shakspere's doughty friends, such a specimen of humanity as Montaigne must have been quite a new and strange phenomenon. They were children of an age which achieved great things because its nobler natures willingly suffered death when the ideals of their life were to be realised. In them, the fire of enthusiasm of the first Reformation, of the glorious time of Elizabeth, was still glowing. They energetically championed the cause of Humanism. The sublime conceptions of their epoch were not yet marred by that dark and gloomy set of men whose mischievous members were just beginning to hatch their hidden plans in the most remote manors of England.

The friends of Shakspere well understood the true meaning of Hamlet's words: [62]--'What should such fellows as I do crawling between earth and heaven?' [63] They easily seized the gist and point of the answer given to the King's question: [64]--'How fares our cousin Hamlet?' when Hamlet replies:--

  Excellent, i' faith; of the chameleon's dish!

Surely, some of them had read the Essay 'On the Inconsistency of our Actions,' and had smiled at the passage:--

'Our ordinary manner is, to follow the inclination of our appetite--this way, that way; upwards, downwards; even as the wind of the occasion drives us. We never think of what we would have, but at the moment we would have it; and we change like that animal (the chameleon) of which it is said that it takes the colour of the place where it is laid down.' [65]

Shakspere's teaching is, that if the nobler-gifted man who stands at the head of the commonwealth, allows himself to be driven about by every wind of the occasion, instead of furthering his better aims with all his strength and energy of will, the wicked, on their part, will all the more easily carry out their own ends. He therefore makes the King say: [66]--

That we would do,
We should do when we would; for this 'would' changes...

Shakspere's friends understood the allusion contained in the first act, after the apparition of the Ghost, when Hamlet calls for his 'tablets.' They knew that the much-scribbling Montaigne was meant, who, as he avows, had so bad a memory that he could not receive any commission without writing it down in his 'tablets' (tablettes). This defect of his, Montaigne mentions over and over again, and may have been the cause of his many most ludicrous contradictions. [67]

After Hamlet has written down the important fact that 'one may smile, and smile, and be a villain--at least, I am sure it may be so in Denmark,' he exclaims:--'Now to my word!' That 'word' undoubtedly consists of the admonition addressed to him by the Ghost, that Hamlet, after having heard his duty, also should fulfil it--that is:--

'So art thou to revenge, when thou shalt hear.'

But he only recollects the last words of the Ghost; and Hamlet's parole, therefore, is only this:--

Adieu, adieu, adieu! Remember me!

The value of Montaigne's book is harshly treated in the second scene of the second act. To the question of Polonius as to what he is reading, Hamlet replies:--'Words, words, words!' Indeed, Shakspere did not think it fair that 'the satirical rogue' should fill the paper with such remarks (whole Essays of Montaigne consist of similar useless prattle) as 'that old men have grey beards; that their faces are wrinkled; their eyes purging thick amber and plum-tree gum; and that they have a plentiful lack of wit, together with most weak hams.' [68]

The ideas of Shakspere as to the duties of a writer were different, indeed, from the contents of the book which Hamlet characterises by his exclamation.

As to Polonius' answer: 'Though this be madness, yet there's method in it,' the public had no difficulty in finding out what was meant by that 'madness,' and to whom it applied.

What may the great master have thought of an author who, as Montaigne does, jots down everything in kaleidoscopic manner, just as changeful accident brings it into his head? In Essay III. (2) we read:--

> 'I cannot get a fixed hold of my object. It moves
> and reels as if with a natural drunkenness. I just seize
> it at some point, such as I find it at the moment, when I
> amuse myself with it. I do not describe its essence, but
> its volatile passage ... from one minute to the other.'

Elsewhere he prides himself on his method of being able to write as long as there is paper and ink.

Hamlet says to the players: 'We'll e'en to it like French falconers: fly at anything we see.' Montaigne's manner of spying out and pouncing upon things cannot be better depicted than by comparing it with a French falconer's manner. In the first act already, Hamlet, after the ghost-scene, answers the friends who approach, with the holla-call of a falconer:--

Hillo, ho, ho, boy; come, bird, come!

Furthermore, Hamlet says in act ii. sc. 2:--'I am but mad north-north-west. When the wind is southerly, I know a hawk from a handshaw (heronshaw!).' Now, the north-west wind would drive Montaigne back into his native province, Perigord, where, very likely according to Shakspere's view, he ought to have remained with his sham logic. The south wind, on the contrary, brings the able falconer to England. The latter possesses such a penetrating glance for the nature of things as to be able to distinguish the bird (the heronshaw) that is to be pursued from the hawk that has been unhooded and cast.

In the second scene of the fifth act, between Hamlet and Horatio (to the weak-minded Osrick the words spoken there are incomprehensible), the excellent qualities of Laertes are apparently judged. [69] This whole discussion is meant against Montaigne; and in the first quarto the chief points are wanting. Florio calls Montaigne's Essays 'Moral, Political, and Military Discourses.' [70] Osrick praises the qualities of the cavalier who has returned from France; and Hamlet replies that 'to divide him inventorily would dizzy the arithmetic of memory.'

The further, hitherto utterly unexplained, words ('and yet but yaw neither in respect of his quick sail') seem to have reference to the sonnet [71] by which the third book of the Essays is dedicated by Florio to Lady Grey. Montaigne is praised therein under the guise of Talbot's name, who, 'in peace or war, at sea or land, for princes' service, countries' good, sweetly sails before the wind.' In act ii. sc. 2, the north-north-west and the south wind were already alluded to, which are said to influence Hamlet's madness.

The translators and admirers of Montaigne are meant when Hamlet says that 'to make true diction of him, his semblable' must be 'his mirror; and, who else would trace him, his umbrage--nothing more.' That is, one must be Montaigne, or become his absolute admirer, 'his umbrage,' 'his semblable,' in order to do justice to him. The whole scene is full of allusions, easily explainable from the point of view we have indicated. So also, the reference to self-knowledge ('to know himself) --an art which Montaigne never learnt and the 'two weapons' with which he fights, are full of deep meaning.

It was probably no small number of men that took delight in the French essayist. No doubt, the jest of the gravedigger is directed against them, when he says that if the mad Hamlet does not recover his wits in England, it is no great matter there, because there the men are as mad as he.

Montaigne, especially in Essay III. (2) and III. (5), brings forward indecencies of the most shameless kind. We quite bear in mind what period it was when he wrote. Our manners and ideas are totally different from those of the sixteenth century. But what indignation must Shakspere have felt--he who had already created his noblest female characters, Helena and Olivia; and who had sung his paean of love, 'Romeo and Juliet'--when he read the ideas of the French nobleman about love and women! Nowhere, and on no occasion, does Shakspere in his dramas, in spite of phrases which to-day we qualify as obscene ones, lower the ideal of the womanly character--of the ewig Weibliche.

But let us read Montaigne's view: [72]--

'I find that love is nothing else than a thirst of enjoying a desired subject; nor that Venus is anything else but the pleasure of emptying one's seminary vessels, similar to the pleasure which Nature has given us in discharging other parts.'

Now, this significant quality also, of saying indecencies without shame, Hamlet has in common with Montaigne. No character in Shakspere's dramas uses such language as Hamlet; and in this case, let it be observed, it is not used between men, but towards the beloved one! We shall remark upon his relations with Ophelia later on.

The frivolous Montaigne speaks of love as one might do of a good dish to be enjoyed at every degree of age, according to taste and inclination. In Essay III.(4) we learn how, in his youth, 'standing in need of a vehement diversion for the sake of distraction, he made himself amorous by art and study.' Elsewhere he tells what great things he was able, as a young man, to achieve in this line. [73] He, therefore, does not agree with the sage who praises age because it frees us from voluptuousness. [74]

He, on the contrary, says:--'I shall never take kindly to impotence, whatever good it may do me.'

Montaigne, the old and young lover, is lashed in act v. sc. I, in disfigured verses of a song sung by the grave-digger, which dates about from the year 1557, and at Shakspere's time probably was very popular. In the original, where the image of death is meant to be represented, an old man looks back in repentance, and with great aversion, upon his youthful days when he found pleasure in love. The original verse stood thus:--

> I lothe that I did love,
> In youth that I thought swete,
> As time requires for my behove,
> Methinks they are not mete.

Until now, no sense could be made of the first verse which the gravedigger sings. It runs thus:--

> In youth, when I did love, did love,

Methought it was very sweet,
To contract, OH! the time, for, AH! my behove,
O, methought, there was nothing meet.

Let it be observed what stress is laid on the 'Oh!'--the proper time, and the 'Ah!'--the delight felt at the moment of enjoyment. The meaning of the old verse is changed in such a manner as to show that old Montaigne looks back with pleasure upon the time of his dissolute youth, whilst the author of the original text shrinks back from it.

The second verse [75] is a further persiflage of the old song. Its reading, too, is changed. It is said there that age, with his stealing steps, as clawed the lover in his clutch [76] and shipped him into the land as if he 'never had been such.'

By none has the relation between Ophelia and Hamlet been better felt and described than by Goethe. He calls her 'the good child in whose soul, secretly, a voice of voluptuousness resounds.' Hamlet who--driven rudderless by his impulse, his passion, his daimon, from one extreme to the other--drags everything that surrounds him into the abyss, also destroys the future of the woman that might truly make him happy. He disowns and rejects her whom Nature has formed for love. At a moment when
fanatical thoughts have mastered his reason, he bids her go to a nunnery.

Once more we must point to the Essay in which Montaigne lays down his ideas about woman and love. French ladies, he says, study Boccaccio and such-like writers, in order to become skilful (habiles). 'But there is no word, no example, no single step in that matter which they do not know better than our books do. That is a knowledge bred in their very veins ... Had not this natural violence of their desires been somewhat bridled by the fear and a feeling of honour wherewith they have been provided, we would be dishonoured (diffamez).' Montaigne says he knows ladies who would rather lend their honour than their 'coach.' [77]

'At last, when Ophelia has no longer any power over her own mind,' says Goethe, 'her heart being on her tongue, that tongue becomes a traitor against her.' [78]

In the scene of Ophelia's madness, we hear songs, thoughts, and phrases probably caught up by her from Hamlet. The ideal which man forms of woman, is the moral altitude on which she stands. Now, let the language be called to mind, which Hamlet, before the players' scene, uses towards his beloved!

Ophelia's words: 'Come, my coach [79]' will be understood from the passage in Montaigne above quoted. The meaning of: 'Oh, how the wheel becomes it!' has reference to a thought developed by Montaigne in Essay III. (11), [80] which we cannot render here, as it is opposed to every feeling of decency.

All commentators agree in thinking that the character of Laertes is in direct contrast to that of Hamlet. In the first quarto, the figure of Laertes is but rapidly indicated. Only that scene is worked out where he cries out against the priest who will not follow his sister to the grave:--

  A ministering angel shall my sister be.
  When thou liest howling.

In the second quarto only, we meet with the most characteristic speeches in which the strong-willed Laertes, [81] unmindful of any future world, calls for revenge with every drop of his indignant blood:--

  To Hell, allegiance! Vows, to the blackest devils!

> Conscience and grace, to the profoundest pit!
> I dare damnation....
> ... Both the worlds I give to negligence,
> Let come what comes ...
> ... to cut his throat i' the church.

That passage, too, is new, in which Ophelia's madness is explained as the consequence of blighted love:--

> Nature is fine in love, and where 't is fine,
> It sends some precious instance of itself
> After the thing it loves.

Her own reason, which succumbs to her love, is the precious token.

In the same way, those words are not in the first quarto, in which Laertes gives vent to the oppressed feelings of his heart, on hearing of the death of his sister:--

> Nature her custom holds,
> Let shame say what it will. When these (the tears) are gone,
> The woman will be out.

All those beautiful precepts, also, which Laertes gives to his sister, are wanting in the quarto of 1603. [82]

Hamlet is the most powerful philosophical production, in the domain of poetry, written at the most critical epoch of mankind--the time of the Reformation. The greatest English genius recognised that it was everyone's duty to set a time out of joint to right. Shakspere showed to his noble friends a gifted and noble man whose life becomes a scourge for him and his surroundings, because he is not guided by manly courage and conscience, but by superstitious notions and formulas.

This colossal drama ranges from the thorny, far-stretching fields which man, only trusting in himself, has to work with the sweat of his brow, to that wonder-land of mystery--

  Where these good tidings of great joy are heard. [83]

If the principles that are fought out in this drama, in tragic conflict, were to be described by catchwords, we might say: Reason stands against Dogma; Nature against Tradition; Self-Reliance against Submission. The great elementary forces are here at issue, which the Reformation had unchained, and with which we all have to reckon.

Shakspere's loving, noble heart beautifully does justice to the defeated Hamlet by making him be borne to his grave 'like a soldier,' with all the honouring 'rites of war.' The poet who knew the human heart so well, no doubt had seen many brave and gifted men who, after having been to Wittenberg's Halls of Intellectual Freedom, and become disciples of Humanism, once more were turned into slaves of dogmas which, under a new guise, not less restricted the free use of reason than the tenets of the old faith had done:--

  Sure, he that made us with such large discourse,
  Looking before and after, gave us not
  The capability and god-like reason
  To fust in us unused.

The life of the most gifted remains fruitless if, through fear of what may befall us in a future world, we cravenly shrink back from following the dictates of our reason and our conscience. From them we must take the mandate and commission for the task of our life; not from any mysterious messenger, nor from any ghost out of Purgatory. On the way to action, no 'goblin damned' must be allowed to cross our path with his assumed terrors. That which we feel to be right we must do, even if 'it be the very witching time of night, and hell breathes contagion into the world.'

Shakspere broke with all antiquated doctrines. He was one of the foremost Humanists in the fullest and noblest meaning of the word. [84]

Notes:
1: Essay II. 12.
2: Essay I. 26.
3: The whole contents of this chapter may be said to be condensed into two lines of Shakspere:--
   'There are more things in heaven and earth, Horatio,
   Than are dreamt of in your philosophy.'
4: Essay III. 13.
5: See Bacon's Essay 'Of Simulation and Dissimulation,' where he says that 'dissimulation followeth many times upon secrecy by a necessity: so that he that will be secret must be a dissembler in some degree,' &c.
6: The following are Hamlet's modes of asseveration:--
   'Angels and ministers of grace,' 'All you host of Heaven,' 'God's love,' 'God and mercy,' 'God's willing,' 'Help and mercy,' 'God's love,' 'By St. Patrick,' 'God-a-mercy,' 'By my fay (ma foi),'
   'S' blood (God's blood),' 'S' wounds,' 'God's bodykins,' 'By'r Lady,' 'Perdy (Pardieu),' 'By the rood (Cross),' 'Heavenly guards,' 'For love and grace,' 'By the Lord,' 'Pray God,' &c.
7: New Shakspere Society (Stubbs, Abuses in England), 1879, p. 131.
8: Act ii. sc. 2.
9: Act ii. sc. i.
10: This description is wanting in the first quarto. The passages there are essentially different; there is no allusion to Hamlet's mental struggle.
11: About various allusions and satirical hints in this scene later on.

12: Florio, 21; Montaigne, I. ii.
13: Essay III. i.
14: Isaiah, ch. iii. v. 16.
15: The word 'ecstasy,' which is often used in the new quarto, is wanting in the first edition where only madness, lunacy, frenzy--the highest degrees of madness--are spoken of.
16: In the old play their names are 'Rosencroft' and 'Guilderstone.'
Reynaldo, in the first quarto, is called 'Montano.'
This change of name in a dramatis persona of minor importance indicates, in however a trifling manner, that the interest excited by the name of Montaigne (to which 'Montano' comes remarkably near in English pronunciation) was now to be concentrated on another point.
17: Essay I. 40.
18: II. 12.
19: Essay II. 27, p. 142.
20: Essay III. 4, p. 384.
21: Rather sharp translations of songe-creux, as Montaigne calls himself (Florio, i. 19, p. 34). 'I am given rather to dreaming and sluggishness.'
22: ''S wounds' (God's wounds)--a most characteristic expression; used by Shakspere only in Hamlet, in this scene, and again in act v. sc. 2.
23: As yet, Hamlet has but one ground of action--namely, the one which, after the apparition of the Ghost, he set down in his tablets: 'that one may smile, and smile, and be a villain; at least, I am sure, it may be so in Denmark.'
24: Act ii. sc. 2.
25: Essay I. 19.
26: II. 3.
27: Tacitus, annal. xiii. 56.
28: Essay I. 19.
29: Act. i. sc. 2.
30: Shakspere already uses this expression in King John (1595) for

purposes of mirthful mockery. He makes the Bastard say to the Archduke of Austria (act iii. sc. i):--'Hang a calf's skin on those recreant limbs!'--a circumstance which convinces us that Shakspere knew the Essays of Montaigne from the original at an early time. We think it a fact important enough to point out that Florio translates peau d'un veau by 'oxe-hide' (fo. 34). We cannot think of any other explanation than that the phrase in question had become so popular through King John as to render it advisable for Florio to steer clear of this rock. Jonson, in his Volpone (act. i. sc. i), makes Mosca the parasite say in regard to his master: 'Covered with hide, instead of skin.'

31: Florio's translation: 'If it be a consummation of one's being' (p. 627). Shakspere: 'a consummation devoutly to be wished.' This word is only once used by Shakspere in such a sense. It occurs in another sense in King Lear (iv. 6) and Cymbeline (iv. 2), but nowhere else in his works.

32: Monologue of the first quarto:--

'To be, or not to be, I there's the point,
To Die, to sleepe, is that all? I all:
No, to sleepe, to dreame, I, mary there it goes,
For in that dreame of death, when wee awake,
And borne before an everlasting judge,
From whence no passenger ever returned,
The undiscovered country, at whose sight
The happy smile, and the accursed damned.
But for this, the joyful hope of this,
Whol'd beare the scornes of flattery of the world,
Scorned by the right rich, the rich curssed of the poore?
The widow being oppress'd, the orphan wronged,
The taste of hunger, or a tyrants raigne,
And thousand more calamities besides,
To grunte and sweate under the weary life,
When that he may his full quietus make,

Shakspere And Montaigne 109

    With a bare bodkin, who would this indure,
    But for a hope of something after death?
    Which pushes the brain and doth connfound the sence,
    Which makes us rather beare those evilles we have,
    Than flie to others that we know not of.
    I that, O this conscience makes cowardes of us all.
    Lady in thy orizons, be all my sinnes remembered.

33: On closely examining the copy of Montaigne's Essays in the British Museum, which bears Shakspere's autograph on the title-page, we found--long after our treatise had been completed--that on the fly-leaf at the end of the volume is written: Mors incrta, (Written somewhat indistinctly, meaning probably *incerta*. It might also be an abbreviation of 'incertam horam' [incr. ho.], as contained in the Latin verse on p. 626:--

  Incertam frustra, mortales, funeris horam
    Quaeritis, et qua sit mors aditura via.)

626, 627. These two numbers, apparently, refer to the corresponding pages of Montaigne's work, which contain nothing but thoughts about the uncertainty of the hour of death and the hereafter. On p. 627 there is the speech of Sokrates, which in Florio's translation, as shown above, bears such striking resemblance to Hamlet's monologue. There are other Latin sentences on the same fly-leaf, pronounced by Sir Frederic Madden to be written by a later pen than Shakspere's. To us, at any rate, the above words and numbers appear to proceed from a different hand than the other sentences. Judgments thereon from persons well versed in the writings of that time would be of great interest.

34: P. 103.

35: I. 19.

36: Act iii. sc. 2.

37: III. 12 (Florio, 626).

38: We do not doubt that this is a sly thrust at Florio, who, in the preface to his translation, calls himself 'Montaigne's Vulcan,' who hatches out Minerva from that 'Jupiter's bigge brain'.

39: Florio, 476.

40: Florio, 592: 'Thus goe the world, and so goe men.'

41: III. 1.

42: II. 27.

43: Clarendon: 'Circumstance of thought' means here the details over which thought ranges, and from which its conclusions are formed.

44: 'Index,' in our opinion, does not signify here either the title, or prologue, or the indication of the contents of a book, but is an allusion to the Index of the Holy See and its thunders.

45: Montaigne, III. 10; Florio, 604: 'Custome is a second nature, and no less powerfull.... To conclude, I am ready to finish this man, not to make another. By longe custome this forme is changed into substance, Fortune into Nature.'

46: III. 1.

47: This is wanting in the first quarto, like the whole conclusion of this scene.

48: This whole scene between Horatio and Hamlet consists of the following four lines in the old quarto:--

> Hamlet. Beleeuve me, it greeuves me much, Horatio,
> That to Laertes I forgot myselfe:
> For by myselfe methinkes I feel his greefe,
> Though there's a difference in each other's way.

Does this not look like a draught destined to be the kernel of a scene? The end of the scene where Osrick comes in, is also much shorter in the older play.

49: Florio, 330: 'We amend ourselves by privation of reason and by her drooping.' Hamlet's conduct is only to be explained by his quietly sitting down until his reason should droop.--II. 12.

50: Florio, 608.

51: Florio, 609.

52: This whole scene is nearly new (in the first quarto it is a mere sketch). There are in it several direct allusions to Montaigne's book, on which we shall touch later on.

53: Here the dramatist, in order to paint a trait of vanity in Hamlet's character, uses a device. He makes the latter say that, since Laertes went into France, he (Hamlet) has been in continual practice. Yet we know (act ii. sc. 2) that he had given up his accustomed exercise. In that scene the poet wishes to describe Hamlet's melancholy; in the other, his vanity. He chooses the colours which are apt to produce quickest impressions among the audience.

54: Act v. sc. 2.

55: See St. Matthew x.29.

56: I. 19.

57: III. 9.

58: II. 12.

59: The Queen describes Hamlet as 'fat, and scant of breath.' Here is Montaigne's description of himself (Essai II. 27):--'J'ay, au demourant, la taille forte et ramassee; le visage non pas gras, mais plein, la complexion entre le jovial et le melancholique, moyennement sanguine et chaude.' Florio's translation, p. 372:--'As for me, I am of a strong and well compact stature, my face is not fat, but full, my complexion betweene joviall and melancholy, indifferently sanguine and hote--('not spleneative and rash').

60: III. 13

61: III. 9.

62: Act iii. sc. 1.

63: We shall now oftener touch upon satirical passages uttered by the character himself against whom they are directed. The true dramatist gives the public no time to think over an incident in full leisure. Every means--as we have already shown before--is welcome to him, which aids in rapidly bringing out the telling traits of his figures. No surprise need therefore be felt that Hamlet, though representing Montaigne, sneers at, and morally flagellates, himself.

64: Act iii. sc. 2.

65: II. 1.

66: Act iv. sc. 7.

67: I. 9, 25; II. 10, &c. If an attentive reader will take the trouble to closely examine that part of the scene in Shakspere's Tempest (act ii. sc. 1) wherein the passage occurs, which he borrowed from Essay I. 30--'On Cannibals'--and compare it with this most 'strange Essay,' he will clearly convince himself that Shakspere can only have made use of it as a satire on Montaigne's defective memory, which entangles this author in the most ludicrous contradictions. Gonzala declares that, if he were king of the isle on which he and his companion were wrecked, he would found a commonwealth as described in the above passage. He concludes this description, saying he would have 'no sovereignty.'
Sebastian justly remarks: 'Yet he would be king on't;' and Antonio continues by saying: 'The latter end of his commonwealth forgets the beginning.'
Even such is the contradiction in Montaigne's fanciful Essay 'On Cannibals,' where, towards the end, he speaks of a captain who holds authority over these savages, not only in war, but also in peace, 'that when he went to visit the village of his dependence, they cut him paths through the thick of their woods, through which he might pass at ease.' The beginning of this Essay described the commonwealth of these cannibals as tolerating no politic superiority, no use of service, no occupation, &c. 'What short memory! much wanting tablets!'
In the above-mentioned scene of the Tempest Sebastian makes the remark: 'No marrying 'mong his subjects,' which evidently is also meant as a hit against Montaigne's anti-matrimonial ideas, which we dwelt upon in the scene between Hamlet and Ophelia.

68: Jonson, long afterwards, had not forgotten this hit against Montaigne. In Epicoene (1609) he makes Cleremont say:--'When we come to have grey heads and weak hams, moist eyes and shrunk members ... then we'll pray and fast.'

69: This whole passage of act v. sc. 2 (106-138) is again only to be found in the quarto of 1604, not in the folio edition of 1623. In later years the poet may have struck it out, as being only comprehensible to a smaller circle of his friends. In the same way that passage of act iv. sc. 4, which only contains thoughts of Montaigne, was not received into the folio of 1623.

70: This is their title in Florio's translation: Morall, Politike, Millitarie Discourses of Lo. Michaell de Montaigne, Knight of the noble order of Saint Michaell, and one of the Gentlemen in ordinary of the French King Henry III. his Chamber.

71: The sonnet runs thus:--

> To the Right Honourable Ladie Elizabeth Grey. (She was a
> daughter of Count Shrewsbury, a Talbot.)
> Of honorable TALBOT honored farre,
> The forecast and the fortune, by his WORD
> Montaigne here descrives; what by his Sword,
> What by his wit; this, as the guiding starre;
> That, as th' Aetolian blast, in peace or warre,
> At sea, or land, as cause did use afforde,
> Avant le vent, to tacke his sails aboarde,
> So as his course no orethwart crosse might barre,
> But he would sweetly sail before the wind;
> For Princes service, Countries good, his fame.
> Heire-Daughter of that prudent, constant kinde,
> Joyning thereto of GREY as great a name, Of
> both chief glories shrining in your minde,
> Honour him that your Honor doth proclaime.'

We have already learned from the preface of the first book of the Essais how Florio was 'sea-tosst, weather-beaten,' 'ship-wrackt,' 'almost drowned,' when exerting himself to capture the whale--Montaigne--and drag him through 'the rocke-rough Ocean' with the assistance of his colleague Diodati, whom he compares to 'a guide-fish.' Hamlet calls Polonius a fish-monger. The latter fools Hamlet by pretending that yonder cloud is in the shape of a whale, which just before appeared to him like the back of a weasel. Every word almost in this wonderful drama is a well-directed hit.

72: Essay III. 5.
73: Ibid. 13.
74: Ibid. 2.
75: The quarto of 1623 has only the third verse.
76: The old song has the word 'crouch.'
77: Essay III. 5, p. 460. Florio, p. 529.
78: We think it is worth while to quote the following verse Montaigne (III. 5) mentions when speaking of that nature of woman, which he thinks suggests to her every possible act of libidinousness:--

Nec tantum niveo gavisa est ulla columbo
Compar, vel si quid dicitur improbius,
Oscula mordenti semper decerpere rostro,
Quantum praecipue multivola est mulier.

Florio translates (514):--

No Pigeons hen, or paire, or what worse name
You list, makes with hir Snow-white cock such game,
With biting bill to catch when she is kist,
As many-minded women when they list.

Is not this the character of Ophelia, as described by Shakspere--the virgin inclining to voluptuousness in Goethe's view?

79: Hamlet, act iv. sc. 5. In *Eastward Hoe*, Marston, Chapman, and Jonson make capital out of this word, and use it as a sneer against Hamlet and Ophelia. We shall return to this point later on.
80: Florio, 617.
81: Act iv. sc. 5.
82: Laertes, act i. sc. 3:--

For nature crescent does not grow alone
In thews and bulk, but, as this temple waxes,
The inward service of the mind and soul

Grows wide withal.
  Montaigne, II. 12; Florio, 319:
   The mind is with the body bred we do behold,
   It jointly growes with it, it waxeth old.--Lucr. xliii. 450.
83: Goethe's Faust.
84: We must mention that John Sterling, in an essay on Montaigne
  (Westminster Review, 1838), makes the following introductory
  remarks:--'On the whole, the celebrated soliloquy in Hamlet
  presents a more characteristic and expressive resemblance to much of
  Montaigne's writings than any other portion of the plays of the great
  dramatist which we at present remember, though it would doubtless be
  easy to trace many apparent transferences from the Frenchman into the
  Englishman's works, as both were keen and many-sided observers in the
  same age and neighbouring countries. But Hamlet was in those days no
  popular type of character; nor were Montaigne's views and tone
  familiar to men till he himself had made them so. Now, the Prince
  of Denmark is very nearly a Montaigne, lifted to a higher eminence,
  and agitated by more striking circumstances and severer destiny,
  and altogether a somewhat more passionate structure of man. It is
  not, however, very wonderful that Hamlet, who was but a part of
  Shakspere, should exhibit to us more than the whole of Montaigne,
  and the external facts appear to contradict any notion of a French
  ancestry for the Dane, as the play is said to have been produced
  in 1600, and the translation of the English not for three years later.'
  During our long search through the Commentaries written on
  Hamlet, we also met with the following treatise: 'HAMLET;
  ein Tendenzdrama Sheakspeare's (sic!!) gegen die skeptische
  und kosmopolitische Weltanschauung des Michael de Montaigne, von G.
  F. Stedefeld, Kreisgerichtsrath. Berlin, 1871.'
  The author of the latter-mentioned little book holds it to be
  probable that Shakspere wrote his Hamlet for the object
  of freeing himself from the impressions of the famous French sceptic.
  He regards this masterwork as 'the Drama of the Doubter;' as 'the

apotheosis of a practical Christianity.' Hamlet, he says, is wanting in Christian piety. He has no faith, no love, no hope. His last words, 'The rest is silence,' show that he has no expectation of a future life. He must perish because he has given up the belief in a divine government of the world and in a moral order of things. We believe we have read the Essays of Michel Montaigne with great attention. We not only do not regard him as a 'sceptic' in the sense meant by Mr. Stedefeld, but we hold him, as well as Hamlet, to be an adherent of the so-called 'practical Christianity' --at least, of what both Montaigne and Hamlet reckon to be such. This 'practical Christianity,' however, is a notion somewhat difficult to define.

V.

THE CONTROVERSY BETWEEN BEN JONSON AND DEKKER.

MENTION OF A DISPUTE BETWEEN BEN JONSON AND SHAKSPERE IN 'THE RETURN FROM PARNASSUS.'

CHARACTERISTIC OF BEN JONSON.

BEN JONSON'S HOSTILE ATTITUDE TOWARDS SHAKSPERE.

DRAMATIC SKIRMISH BETWEEN BEN JONSON AND SHAKSPERE.

BEN JONSON'S 'POETASTER.'

DEKKER'S 'SATIROMASTIX.'

We now proceed to an inquiry into the 'controversy between Jonson and Dekker,' which has been repeatedly mentioned before.

Shakspere, we shall find, was implicated in it in a very large degree. Instead of indicating, however, that controversy by the designation under which it is known in literature, it would be more correct to put SHAKSPERE'S name in the place of that of Dekker. Many a reader who perhaps does not fully trust yet our bold assertion that Hamlet is a counterfeit of Montaigne's individuality, will now, we hope, be convinced by vouchers drawn from dramas published in 1604 and 1605, and which are in the closest connection with that controversy. We intend partly making a thorough examination of, partly consulting in a cursory manner, the following pieces:--

1. 'Poetaster' (1601), by Ben Jonson.
2. 'Satiromastix' (1602), by Thomas Dekker.
3. 'Malcontent' (1604), by John Marston.
4. 'Volpone' (1605), by Ben Jonson.
5. 'Eastward Hoe' (1605), by Ben Jonson, Chapman, and Marston.

In 'The Poetaster' Ben Jonson makes his chief attack upon Dekker and Shakspere. In 'Satiromastix,' Dekker defends himself against that attack. In doing so, he sides with Shakspere; and we thereby gain an insight into the noble conduct of the latter. Between Jonson and Shakspere there had already been dramatic skirmishes during several years before the appearance of 'The Poetaster.' We shall only be able to touch rapidly upon their meaning, considering that we confine ourselves, in the main, to a statement of that which concerns 'Hamlet.'

After Jonson, in his 'Poetaster,' had exceeded all bounds of decent behaviour with most intolerable arrogance, Shakspere seems to have become weary of these malicious personal onslaughts; all the more so because they were apparently put into the mouth of innocent children. So he wrote his 'Hamlet,' showing up, therein, the loose and perplexing ideas of his chief antagonist, who belonged to the party of Florio-Montaigne.

Hamlet, as we shall prove beyond the possibility of cavil, is the hitherto unexplained 'purge' in 'The Return from Parnassus,' which 'our fellow Shakspere' administered to Ben Jonson in return for the 'pill' destined for himself in 'The Poetaster.' After the publication of 'Hamlet,' Jonson wrote his 'Volpone' as a counterblast to this drama. Now 'Volpone,' and the Preface in which the author dedicates it to the two Universities, furnish us with the evidence that our theory must be a fact; for Jonson therein defended both the party of Florio-Montaigne and himself.

Moreover, we shall adduce a series of proofs from 'The Malcontent' and from 'Eastward Hoe.'

A drama, written by an unknown author, and printed in 1606, offers us a valuable material wherewith to make it clear that, at that time, a very bitter feud must have raged between Jonson and Shakspere; for it is scarcely to be believed that it would have been brought on the stage had a larger public not been deeply interested in the controversy. 'The Return from Parnassus, or the Scourge of Simony,' [1] is the title of the play, mentioned several times before, in which this controversy is referred to in clear words. Philomusus and Studioso, two poor scholars who in vain had sought to pursue their calling as medical men, resolve upon going to the more profitable stage. They are to be prepared for it by two of the most famous actors from the Globe Theatre (Shakspere's company), Burbage and Kemp. Whilst these are waiting for their new pupils, [2] they converse about the capabilities of the students for the histrionic art. Kemp, in words which show that the author must have had great knowledge of the stage, condemns their ways and manners, mocking the silly kind of acting which he had once seen in a performance of the students at Cambridge. Burbage thinks they might amend their faults in course of time, and that, at least, advantage could be taken of them in so far as to make them write a part now and then; which certainly they could do. To this Kemp replies:--

'Few of the University pen plaies well; they smell too much of that writer Ovid *and that writer* Metamorphosis, and talk too much of Proserpina *and* Jupiter. Why, here's our fellow Shakespeare puts them all down--I, and Ben Jonson *too. O that* Ben Jonson is a pestilent fellow; he brought up Horace giving the poets a pill; [3] but our fellow Shakespeare hath given him spurge that made him bewray his credit.'

Burbage answers:--'It's a shrewd fellow indeed.'

For the better understanding of this most interesting controversy, the centre of which Hamlet forms, it is necessary that we should give a characteristic of Shakspere's adversary, Ben Jonson, whose individuality and mode of action are too little known among the general reading public.

Ben Jonson, born in 1573, in the neighbourhood of Westminster, was the posthumous child of a Scot who had occupied a modest position at the Court of Henry VIII., but who, under Queen Mary, had to suffer long imprisonment, probably on account of his religious opinions. His estates were confiscated by the Crown. After having obtained his liberation, he became a priest of the Reformed Church of England. Two years after his death, his widow, the mother of Ben, again married: this time her husband was a master bricklayer. The education of the boy from the first marriage, who at an early age showed talent for learning, was not neglected. It is assumed that friends of his father, seeing Ben's ability, rendered it possible for him to enter Westminster School, and afterwards to study at the University of Cambridge. In his seventeenth or eighteenth year, probably from a want of means, he had to give up the career of learning, in order to follow the simple calling of his stepfather. It may be easily understood that Ben was little pleased with the use of the trowel; he fled to the Netherlands, became a soldier, and took part in a campaign. After a year, the youthful adventurer, then only nineteen years old, came back to London. He talks of a heroic deed; but the truthfulness of his account may well be doubted. He pretends having killed an enemy, in the face of both camps, and come back to the ranks, laden with his spoils.

After his return to London, Jonson first tried to earn his livelihood as an actor. His figure [4] and his scorbutic face were, however, sad hindrances to his success. Soon he gave up the histrionic attempts and began to write additions to existing plays, at the order of a theatrical speculator, of the name of Philip Henslowe. The only further detail we have of Jonson's doings, down to 1598, [5] is, that he fell out with one of his colleagues, an actor (Jonson's quarrelsome disposition as regards his comrades commenced very early), and that finally he killed his antagonist. We then find him in prison where a Catholic priest induced him to become a convert to the Roman Church which, after the lapse of about twelve years, he again left, returning to the Established Protestant Church of England. Jonson himself afterwards said once that 'he was for any religion, as being versed in both.' [6] It is, therefore, not to be assumed that he once more changed from conviction. His reconversion appears rather to have been a prudential act on his part, in order to conform to the religious views of the pedantic James I., and thus to obtain access at Court, which aim he indeed afterwards reached; whereas he had not been able to obtain that favour under Elizabeth. [7]

It is not known by what, or by whom, Ben Jonson was saved from the near prospect of the gallows. In 1598 his name is mentioned as one of the better-known writers of comedies, by Francis Meres, in his 'Palladis Tamia.' His first successful comedy was, 'Every Man in his Humour.' Fama says that the manuscript which the author had sent in to the Lord Chamberlain's Company, was on the point of being rejected when Shakspere requested to have the play given to him, read it, and caused its being acted on the stage. This anecdote belongs, however, to the class of traditional tales of that age, whose value for fixing facts is a most doubtful one. It is more certain that Ben, at the age of twenty, took a wife; which contributed very little to the lessening of his chronic poverty with which he constantly had to struggle. It does not appear that the union was a very happy one; for he relates that he once left his wife for five years.

A diary written by an unknown barrister informs us, February 12, 1602: 'Ben Jonson, the poet, nowe lives upon one Townesend and scornes the world.' [8] In the society of gallants and lords, the young poet felt himself most at home. All kinds of mendicant epistles, sonnets, dedications, petitions, and so forth, which he addressed to high personages, and which have been preserved, convince us that Jonson neglected nothing that could give an opportunity to the generosity of liberal noblemen to prove themselves patrons of art in regard to him. He boasts on the stage of being more in the enjoyment of the favour of the great ones than any of his literary contemporaries. [9] Modesty was certainly not a mitigating trait in the character of hot-tempered Jonson, whose wrath was easily roused.

Convinced of the power of his own genius, he most eagerly wanted to see the value of his work acknowledged. Not satisfied with the slow judgment his contemporaries might come to, or the niggardly reward they might confer; nor content with the prospects of a laurel wreath which grateful Posterity lays on the marble heads of departed eminent men, this pretentious disciple of the Muse importunately claimed his full recompense during his own life. For the applause of the great mass, the dramatist, after all, has to contend. Jonson strove hard for it; but in vain. A more towering genius was the favourite of the age. Ben, however, laid the flattering unction to his soul that he was above Shakspere, [10] even as above all other contemporary authors; and he left nothing unattempted to gain the favour of the great public. All his endeavours remained fruitless. On every occasion he freely displays the rancour he felt at his ill-success; for he certainly was not master of his temper. In poems, epistles, and epigrams, as well as in his dramas, and in the dedications, prologues, and epilogues attached thereto, he shows his anger against the 'so-called stage poets.' We shall prove that his fullest indignation is mainly directed against one--the very greatest: need we name him?

Jonson, resolved upon making the most of his Muse in a remunerative sense, well knew how to obtain the patronage of the highest persons of the country; and his ambition seems to have found satisfaction when, afterwards, a call was made upon him, on the part of the Court, to compose 'Masques' for Twelfth-Night and similar extraordinary occasions. He produced a theatrical piece in consonance with the barbaric taste prevailing in Whitehall, which gave plenty to do to the machinists, the decorators, and the play-dresser of the stage. With such a division of labour in the domain of art, it is not easy, to-day, to decide to whom the greater merit belongs, among those concerned, of having afforded entertainment to the courtiers. Dramatic or poetical value is wanting in those productions of Jonson.

From his poems, as well as from the 'Conversations with Drummond,' we know that among the patronesses of Jonson there were Lucie Countess of Bedford and Elizabeth Countess of Rutland--two ladies to whom Florio dedicated a translation of Montaigne. Lady Rutland's marriage was a most unhappy one. In the literary intercourse with prominent men of her time she appears to have sought consolation and distraction.

Jonson's relations with this lady must have been rather friendly ones, for 'Ben one day being at table with my Lady Rutland, her husband coming in, accused her that she keept table to poets, of which she wrott a letter to him (Jonson), which he answered. My lord intercepted the letter, but never chalenged him.' [11]

From the same source which makes this statement we take the following trait in Jonson's character, which is as little calculated as his passionate quarrelsomeness to endear him to us. Sir Thomas Overbury had become enamoured of unhappy Lady Rutland. Jonson was asked by this nobleman, who at the same time was a poet, to read to the adored one a lyrical effusion of his; evidently for the purpose of fomenting her inclinations towards the friend who was languishing for her. Ben Jonson relates that he fulfilled Overbury's wish 'with excellent grace,' at the same time praising the author. Next morning he fell out with Overbury, who would have him to make an unlawful proposal to Lady Rutland.

But how, we may ask, was it possible that Jonson's noble friend could at all think of trying to use him as a go-between in this shameful manner? Are we not reminded here of the position of thirsty Toby Belch towards the simple Aguecheek, if not even of honest [12] Iago in his dealings with the liberal Rodrigo? Neither in Olivia's uncle, nor in Othello's Ancient is it reckoned a merit to have omitted doing pimp service to friends. Their policy of taking advantage of amorous inclinations, although they did not even try to promote them by the reading of poetical productions, remains not the less contemptible.

As to Jonson's passion for the cup that does more than cheer, neither he himself conceals it, nor is evidence to the same effect wanting on the part of his contemporaries. Drayton says that he was in the habit of 'wearing a loose coachman's coat, frequenting the Mermaid Tavern, where he drank seas of Canary; then reeling home to bed, and, after a profuse perspiration, arising to his dramatic studies.' [13]

At a certain time, Jonson accompanied a son of Sir Walter Raleigh as tutor during a voyage to France. The young hopeful pupil, 'being knavishly inclined,' and not less quick in the execution of practical jokes than in spying out human weaknesses, had no difficulty in understanding his tutor's bent, and succeeded in making Jonson 'dead drunk.' He then 'laid him on a carr, which he made to be drawn by pioners through the streets, at every corner showing his governour stretched out, and telling them, that was a more lively image of the Crucifix than any they had.' The mother of young Raleigh greatly relished this sport. It reminded her of similar tricks her husband had been addicted to in his boyish days, 'though the father abhorred it.'

With habits of the kind described, Jonson had a hard but fruitless struggle against oppressing poverty and downright misery during his whole life. When age was approaching, he addressed himself to his highborn patrons with petitions in well-set style. His needy condition was, however, little bettered, even when Charles I., in 1630, conferred upon him, seven years before his death, an annual pension of 100 pounds, with a terse of Spanish wine yearly out of his Majesty's store at Whitehall.

A letter of Sir Thomas Hawkins describes one of the last circumstances of Jonson's life. At 'a solemn supper given by the poet, when good company, excellent cheer, choice wine, and jovial welcome had opened his heart and loosened his tongue, he began to raise himself at the expense of others.'

Wine, joviality, good company, and bitter satire--these were the elements of Ben Jonson's happiness.

'O rare Ben Jonson!' Sir John Young, [14] who, walking through Westminster Abbey, saw the bare stone on the poet's grave, gave one of the workmen eighteenpence to cut the words in question, and posterity is still in doubt whether the word 'rare' was meant for the valuable qualities of the poet or for those of the boon-companion.

We will give a short abstract of Jonson's character from the notes of a contemporary whose guest he had been during fully a month in 1619. One might doubt the sincerity of this judgment if Sir William Drummond, his liberal host, had made it public for the purpose of harming Jonson. There was, however, no such intention, for it remained in manuscript for fully two hundred years.

Only then, a copy of this incisive characteristic came before the world at large. The Scottish nobleman and poet had written it down, together with many utterances of Jonson, after his guest who most freely and severely criticised his contemporaries had left. The perspicacity of Drummond, and the truthful rendering of his impressions, are fully confirmed by Jonson's manner of life and the contents of his literary productions. [15] Drummond concludes his notes thus:--

'He' (Jonson) 'is a great lover and praiser of himself; a contemner and scorner of others; given rather to loose a friend than a jest; jealous of every word and action of those about him (especially after drink, which is one of the elements in which he liveth): a dissembler of ill parts which reigne in him; a bragger of some good that he wanteth; thinking nothing well but what either himself or some of his friends and countrymen have said or done. He is passionately kind and angry; careless either to gain or keep; vindicative, but, if he be well answered, at himself. For any religion, as being versed in both;

interpreteth best sayings and deeds often to the worst. Oppressed with fantasie, which has ever mastered his reason: a general disease in many poets.'

It will easily be understood that between two natures of so opposite a bent as that of the quarrelsome Jonson and 'gentle Shakspere,' friendship for any length of time could scarcely be possible. [16]

The creations of the dramatist obtain their real value by the poet's own character. He who breathes a soul into so many figures destined for action must himself be gifted with a greatness of soul that encompasses a world. In the dramatic art, such actions only charm which are evolved out of clearly defined passions; and such characters only awake interest which bear human features strongly marked. If, however, we cast a glance at the dramatic productions of Ben Jonson, we in vain look among the many figures that crowd his stage for one which could inspire us with sympathy. Time has pronounced its verdict against his creations: they are lying in the archive of mere curiosities. Even the inquirer feels ill at ease when going for them to their hiding-place. Jonson's characters do not speak with the ever unmistakeable and touching voice of human passions. In his comedies he produces the strangest whims, caprices, and crotchets, by which he probably points to definite persons. The clue to these often malignant dialectics is very difficult to find.

The action of his plays--if incidental quarrels, full of sneering allusions, are left aside--is generally of such diminutive proportions that one may well ask, after the perusal of some of his dramas, whether they contain any action at all. No doubt the satirist, too, has his legitimate place in the dramatic art; but he must know how to hit the weaknesses of human nature in certain striking types. Jonson, however, is far from being able to lay a claim to such dramaturgic merit. At 'haphazard he took certain individualities from the idly gossiping crowd that congregated in the central nave of St. Paul's Church, and put them on the stage. Whoever had been strutting about there to-day in his silken stockings, proudly displaying the nodding feathers in his hat, his rich waist-coat and mantle, and boasting a little too loud before some other gallant of his love adventures, ran great danger--like all those whose demeanour in St. Paul's gave rise to backbiting gossip--of being pourtrayed in the 'Rose,' in the 'Curtain,' or in the theatres of the 'little eyases,' in such a manner that people were able, in the streets, to point them out with their fingers.

Like so many other novelties, this kind of comedy, too, may for a while have found its admirers. Soon, however, this degradation of the Muse brought up such a storm that Jonson had to take refuge in another domain of the dramatic art (1601). He himself confesses:--

And since the Comic Muse
Hath proved so ominous to me, I will try
If Tragedy have a more kind aspect. [17]

But he is nothing if not satirical. The persons that are to enliven his tragedies are not filled with the true breath of life. They are mere phantoms or puppets of schoolcraft, laboriously put together by a learning drawn from old folios. In his tragedies, 'Sejanus' and 'Cataline,' he seeks to describe Romans whose whole bearing was to be in pedantically close harmony with the time in which the dramatic action occurs. Only a citizen from a certain period of ancient Rome would be able to decide whether this difficult but thankless problem had been solved. These cold academic treatises--for such we must, practically, take them to be--were not relished by the public. There is no vestige of human passion in the bookish heroes thus put on the stage. For their sorrows the audience has no feeling of fear or anguish and no tear of compassion.

Jonson, indignant at the small estimate in which his arduously composed works were received, ill-humoured by their want of success, looked enviously upon Shakspere, who had not been academically schooled; who audaciously overthrew the customs of the antique drama; who made his own rules, or rather, who made himself a rule to others; who created metrics that were peculiarly his; who chose themes hitherto considered non-permissible, and unusual with Greeks and Romans; who flung the 'three unities' to the winds; and who, nevertheless, had an unheard-of success!

This favourite of the public, Jonson seems to have looked upon as the main obstacle barring the way to his own genius. Against this towering rival, Jonson directed a hail of satirical arrows. Only take, for instance, the prologue to 'Every Man in his Humour.' [18] There, Jonson, with the most arrogant conceit, tries to make short work of various dramas of Shakspere's--for instance, of his historical plays, in which he dared--

> ... with three rusty swords,
> And help of some few foot and half-foot words,
> Fight over York and Lancaster's long jars,
> And in the tyring-house bring wounds to scars.

In 'The Poetaster,' which in 1601 was acted by the children of the Queen's Chapel, Jonson made an attack upon three poets. We hope to be able to prove that the one most bitterly abused, and who is bidden to swallow the 'pill,' is no other than Shakspere, whilst the two remaining ones are John Marston and Thomas Dekker. From the 'Apologetical Dialogue' which Jonson wrote after 'The Poetaster' had already passed over the stage, we see that this satire had excited the greatest indignation and sensation in the dramatic world. It was a new manner of falling out with a colleague before the public. The conceited presumption of the author, who in the play itself assumes the part of Horace, seriously proclaiming himself as the poet of poets, as the worthiest of the worthy, is not less enormous and repulsive than the way in which he proceeds against his rivals.

Quite innocently, Jonson asks in that dialogue (which was spoken on the stage after 'The Poetaster' had given rise to a general squabble), how it came about that such a hubbub was made of that play, seeing that it was free from insults, only containing 'some salt' but 'neither tooth, nor gall,' whilst his antagonists, after all, had been the cause of whatever remarks he himself had made:--

... But sure I am, three years
They did provoke me with their petulant styles,
On every stage. And I at last, unwilling,
But weary, I confess, of so much trouble,
Thought I would try if shame could win upon 'em.

In some comedies of Shakspere, which appeared between the years 1598 and 1601, there are characters markedly stamped with Jonsonian peculiarities. We may be convinced that 'gentle Shakspere' had received many a provocation [19] before he took notice of the obscure dramatist who was younger by ten years than himself, and publicly gave him a strong lesson. 'All's Well that Ends Well' contains a figure, Parolles, whose peculiarities are too closely akin to those of Ben Jonson to be regarded as a mere fortuitous accident; especially when we find that Jonson, in 'The Poetaster,' again tries to ridicule this hit by a characteristic expression. [20]

Parolles is a follower of Count Rousillon. His position is not further defined than that he follows Bertram; he is a cross between a gentleman and a servant. We hear the old Lord Lafeu reproaching him in act ii. sc. 3:--

'Why dost thou garter up thy arms o' this fashion? dost make hose of thy sleeves? Do other servants do so?'

Again he calls him--'a vagabond, no true traveller: you are more saucy with lords and honourable personages than the heraldry of your birth and virtue gives you commission.' [21]

Parolles boasts of being born under the sign of Mars, and up to every heroic deed; and it is certainly an allusion to Jonson's bravado of having in the Low Countries, in the face of both camps, killed an enemy and taken opima spolia from him, that Shakspere lets this character make the attempt to retake, single-handed, from the enemy, a drum that had been lost in the battle. Of course, Parolles finally comes out a coward and a traitor. Parolles also mentions that he understands 'Low Dutch.'

In the character of Malvolio ('Twelfth Night; or What You Will,' 1600-1601), the quarrelsome Ben has long ago been suspected, who, puffed up with braggart pride, contemptuously looks down upon his colleagues, and impudently exerts himself to gain access to high social circles; thus assuming, like Parolles, a position that does not properly belong to him. Even as Lord Lafeu takes Parolles a peg lower, so Sir Toby (act. ii. sc. 3) reminds the haughty Malvolio that he is nothing more than a steward. The religion of Malvolio also is several times discussed. Merry Maria relates that he is a 'Puritan or anything constantly but a time-pleaser.' Nor is the priest wanting who is to drive out the hyperbolical fiend from the captive Malvolio: an unmistakeable allusion to Ben Jonson's conversion in prison. The Fool who represents the Priest, puts a question referring to Pythagoras to Malvolio who is groaning 'in darkness' and yearning for freedom. He receives an evasive answer from the prisoner. In 'Volpone,' as we shall see, Jonson answers it very fully. [22]

Altogether, there are allusions in 'The Poetaster,' and in 'Volpone,' to 'All's Well that Ends Well,' and to 'What You Will,' which we shall have to touch upon in speaking of those plays.

The scene of 'The Poetaster' is laid at the court of Augustus Caesar. Jonson therein describes himself under the character of Horace. The whole drift of the play is, to take the many enemies of the latter to task for their calumnies and libels against him. Rome is the place of action, and the persons of the drama bear classic names. There are, besides Augustus and Horace, Mecaenas (sic), Virgil, Propertius, Trebatius, Ovid, Demetrius Fannius, Rufus Laberius Crispinus, and so forth. The characters whom they are to represent are mostly authors of the dramatic world around Ben Jonson. They are depicted with traits so easily recognisable that--as Dekker says in his 'Satiromastix'--of five hundred people four hundred could 'all point with their fingers in one instant at one and the same man.'

More especially against two disciples of the Muse is Jonson's 'gally ink' directed. Let us give a few instances of the lampoons and calumnious squibs by which Horace pretends having been insulted on the part of envious colleagues who, he maintains, look askance at him because 'he keeps more worthy gallants' company' than they can get into. In act iv. sc. I, Demetrius tells Tucca:--

'Alas, Sir, Horace! he is a mere sponge; nothing but humours and observation; he goes up and down, sucking from every society, and when he comes home, squeezes himself dry again.'

Tucca adds:--'He will sooner lose his best friend than his least jest.'

Crispinus is found guilty of having composed a libel against Horace, of which the following may serve as a specimen:--

Ramp up my genius, be not retrograde;
But boldly nominate a spade a spade.
What, shall thy lubrical and glibbery muse
Live, as she were defunct, like punk in stews?
Alas! that were no modern consequence,
To have cothurnal buskins frighted hence.
No, teach thy Incubus to poetize;
And throw abroad thy spurious snotteries....
O poets all and some! for now we list
Of strenuous vengeance to clutch the fist.

Such was the language the contemporaries of Shakspere used. Are we to wonder, then, if here and there we find in his works an offensive expression?

The two persons who are specially taken to task, and most harshly treated, are Demetrius Fannius, 'play-dresser and plagiarius,' and RUFUS LABERIUS CRISPINUS, 'poetaster and plagiarius.' In 'Satiromastix,' Demetrius clearly comes out as Dekker. Crispinus is the chief character of the play:--'the poetaster.' Against him the satire is mainly directed, and for his sake it seems to have been written, for the title runs thus: 'The Poetaster, or His Arraignment.' From all the characteristic qualities of Crispinus we draw the conclusion that this figure represented SHAKSPERE.

From the above-mentioned passage in 'The Return from Parnassus' it would seem as if a 'pill' had been administered in the play to several poets. That is, however, not so. Then, as now, the plural form was a favourite one with writers afraid to attack openly. Horace administers a pill only to one poet--to Crispinus. And as Kemp says that Shakspere, thereupon, gave a 'purge,' the conclusion is obvious that he who took revenge by administering the purge, must have been the one to whom the pill had been given. 'Volpone,' a play directed against the 'purge'--that is, 'Hamlet'--will convince us that the chief controversy lay between Jonson and Shakspere, and not between Jonson and Dekker.

The following points will, we think, make it still clearer that we are warranted in believing that the figure of Crispinus was intended by Jonson for Shakspere.

When, in presence of Augustus, as well as of the high jurors Maecenas, Tibullus, and Virgil, the two poetasters have been heard; when Horace has forgiven Demetrius, [23] and Crispinus, under the sharp effects of the pill, has thrown up, amidst great pain, [24] the disgraceful words which he had used against Horace, he is dismissed by the latter with the admonition to observe, in future, a strict and wholesome diet; to take each morning something of Cato's principles; then taste a piece of Terence and suck his phrase; to shun Plautus and Ennius as meats too harsh for his weak stomach, and to read the best Greeks, 'but not without a tutor.'

This fits in with Shakspere's 'small Latin and less Greek'--a circumstance of which Jonson himself, in his poem in memory of Shakspere (1623), thought he should remind the coming generations.

It is, no doubt, a little revenge for the 'dark chamber' in which Malvolio [25] is imprisoned, that, after Horace has concluded his speech in which the study of Latin and Greek is recommended to Crispinus as something very necessary for him, Virgil should add the further advice:--

> And for a week or two see him locked up
> In some dark place, removed from company;
> He will talk idly else after his physic.

The full name given by Jonson to Crispinus is--RUFUS LABERIUS CRISPI-

NUS.

John Marston already, in 1598, designates Shakspere with the nickname 'Rufus.' Everyone can convince himself of this by first reading Shakspere's 'Venus and Adonis,' and immediately afterwards John Marston's 'Metamorphosis of Pigmalion's Image.' [26] We do not know whether it has struck anyone as yet that this poem of Marston is a most evident satire, written even in the same metre as Shakspere's first, and at that time most popular, poem. [27] In his sixth satire of 'The Scourge of Villanie,' Marston explains why he had composed his 'Pigmalion's Image:'--

Yet deem'st that in sad seriousnesse I write
such nasty stuff as in Pigmalion?
Such maggot-tainted, lewd corruption! ...
Hence, thou misjudging censor: know I wrot
Those idle rimes to note the odious spot
and blemish that deformes the lineaments
of modern poesies habiliments.

At the end of his satire ('Pigmalion's Image'), Marston self-complacently tacks on a concluding piece: 'The Author in Praise of his Precedent Poem.' Whom else does he address there than him whose poetical manner he wished to mock--namely, Shakspere's--when he begins with these words:--

Now, Rufus! by old Glebron's fearfull mace,
Hath not my Muse deserv'd a worthy place? ...
Is not my pen compleate? Are not my lines
Right in the swaggering humour of these times?

The name of 'Rufus' has two peculiarities which may have induced Marston to confer it upon Shakspere. First of all, like the English king of that name, Shakspere's pre-name was William. Secondly, the best-preserved portrait of Shakspere shows him with hair verging upon a reddish hue.

But not only the colour of the hair, but also its thinness (according to all pictures and busts we have of Shakspere, he was bald-headed), seems to have been satirised by Jonson in his 'Poetaster.' In act ii. sc. 1, Chloe asks Crispinus, who, excited by her love and her beauty, pretends becoming a poet, whether, as a poet, he would also change his hair? To which Crispinus replies, 'Why, a man may be a poet, and yet not change his hair.'

Now Dekker, in his 'Satiromastix, in which all personal insults are to be avenged [28](for which reason the chief personages of 'The Poetaster' are introduced under the same name), makes Horace give forth a long song in praise of 'heades thicke of hair,' whilst Crispinus gives another in honour of 'balde heads;' from which we conclude that Chloe's remark on Crispinus' hair has reference to a bald pate, but the name of 'Rufus' to the colour of whatever hair there is.

'Rufus Laberius Crispinus' might truly be thus rendered: 'The red-haired SHAK-erius, with the crisp-head, who cribs like St. Crispin.' The word Rufus, as already explained, reminds us both of Shakspere's red hair and his pre-name 'William.' Laberius (from labare, to shake; hence Shak-erius, a similar nickname as Greene's SHAKE-scene) is clearly an indication of the poet's family name. The Roman custom of placing the name of the gens, or family, in the middle of a person's name, leaves no doubt as to Jonson's intention. Laberius was a dramatic poet, even as Shakspere. Laberius was an actor (Suet. c.i. 39). So was Shakspere. Laberius played in his own dramas. Shakspere did the same. Laberius' name corresponds etymologically, as regards meaning, to the root-syllable in Shakspere's name. Could Jonson, who was so well versed in classics, have made his satirical allusion plainer or more poignant? In Crispinus, both Shakspere's curly hair and the offence of application, plagiarism, or literary theft, with which he is charged by his antagonist, are manifestly marked; St. Crispin being noted among the saints for his filching habits. He made shoes for the poor from materials stolen from the rich.

Crispinus approaches Horace quite as a 'Johannes Factotum,' as Greene had designated Shakspere in 1592. Jonson makes him assert that he, too, is a scholar, a writer conversant with every kind of poetry, and a Stoic. He also declares that he is studying architecture, and that, if he builds a house, [29] it must be similar to one before which they are standing.

In Dekker's 'Satiromastix,' Crispinus is described as being of a most gentle nature. This is in harmony with the well-known quality generally attributed to Shakspere. In the beginning of 'Satiromastix,' Crispinus approaches Horace for the object of peace and reconciliation. The latter excuses himself, in words similar to those of the 'Apologetical Dialogue,' that even if he should 'dip his pen in distilde Roses,' or strove to drain out of his ink all gall, [30] yet his enemies would look at his writings 'with sharpe and searching eyes.' Nay--

> When my lines are measur'd out as straight
> As even parallels, 'tis strange that still,
> Still some imagine they are drawne awry.
> The error is not mine, but in their eye;
> That cannot take proportions.

> Crispinus. Horrace, Horrace!
> To stand within the shot of galling tongues,
> Proves not your gilt, for could we write on paper,
> Made of these turning leaves of heaven, the cloudes,
> Or speak with Angels tongues: yet wise men know,
> That some would shake the head, tho' saints should sing,

Some snakes must hisse, because they're borne with stings.

Horace. 'T is true.

Crispinus. Doe we not see fooles laugh at heaven? and mocke
The Makers workmanship?

Crispinus goes on telling Horace that none are safe from such calumnies; but that, if his 'dastard wit' will 'strike at men in corners,' if he will 'in riddles folde the vices' of his best friends, then he must expect also that they will 'take off all gilding from their pilles,' and offer him 'the bitter coare' (core). [31] With great emphasis, Crispinus admonishes Horace not to swear that he did not intend whipping the private vices of his friends while his 'lashing jestes make all men bleed.' Crispinus concludes his mild, conciliatory speech with the words:--

We come like your phisitions (physicians) to purge
Your sicke and daungerous minde of her disease.

A peace is then concluded, which Horace (Jonson) again breaks, for which he receives his punishment towards the end of 'Satiromastix.' Dekker, who brings in the chief personages of 'The Poetaster' under the same name, makes, in this counter-piece, two parts of the figure of Rufus Laberius Crispinus--namely, that of William Rufus, the king, at whose court he lays the scene (Jonson's drama has the court of Augustus), and that of Crispinus, the poet. The part of the king is a very unimportant one; and it may be assumed that Dekker intended the king and the poet to be looked upon as the same person. The object of the play-dresser Demetrius (Dekker) was, no doubt, to do homage in this way to his chief Crispinus--that is, Shakspere. When the accused Horace is to be judged, the King says to Crispinus:--

Not under us, but next us take thy seate;
Artes nourished by Kings make Kings more great.

Crispinus declares Horace guilty of having 'rebelled against the sacred laws of divine Poesie,' not out of love of virtue, but--

Thy pride and scorn made her turne saterist.

Horace, on account of his crimes against the sacred laws of divine poesy, is not 'lawrefyed,' but 'nettlefyed:' not crowned with laurels, but with a wreath of nettles, and afterwards, in Sancho Panza manner, tossed in a blanket. He then is told:--'You shall not sit in a Gallery when your Comedies and Enterludes have entred their Actions, and there make vile faces at everie lyne, to make Gentlemen have an eye to you, and to make Players afraide to take your part.' Furthermore, he 'must forsweare to venter on the stage when your Play is ended, and to exchange courtezies and complements with Gallants in the Lordes roomes, to make all the house rise up in Armes, and to cry that's Horace, that's he, that's he, that's he, that pennes and purges Humours and diseases.' He must promise 'not to brag in Bookebinders shops that your Vize-royes or Tributorie Kings have done homage to you, or paide Quarterage.' And--'when your Playes are misse-likt at Court, you shall not Crye Mew like a Pusse-Cat, and say you are glad you write out of the Courtiers Elements.' [32]

In his Preface to 'Satiromastix' ('To the World '), Dekker says that in this play he did 'only whip his (Horace's) fortunes and condition of life, where the more noble **REPREHENSION** had bin of his MINDES DEFORMITIE.' [33]

This nobler reprehension, as we have sufficiently shown, was undertaken by Shakspere in his 'Hamlet.' [34] Dekker, in his Epilogue to 'Satiromastix' (he there speaks of the 'Heretical Libertine Horace'), asks the public for its applause; for Horace would thereby be induced to write a counter-play: which, if they hissed his own 'Satiromastix,' would not be the case. By applauding, they would thus, in fact, get more sport; for we 'will untrusse him agen, and agen, and agen.'

Shakspere may have been tired of this fruitless pastime, of those pitiful squabbles, as appears also from the reproach he makes in 'Hamlet' to his people. By the 'more noble REPREHENSION' which he administered to Jonson and his party, he became absorbed in the profounder problems concerning mankind. The time of the lighter comedies is now past for him. There follow now his grandest master-works. Henceforth the poet stands in a relation created by himself to his God and to the world.

We proceed to an examination of 'Volpone,' of that play which Jonson sent as a counter-thrust after 'Hamlet,' and from which, as regards our Hamlet-Montaigne theory, we hope to convince our readers in the clearest manner possible.

Notes:
1: Arber's English Scholars Library, 1879, shows that this highly interesting drama was for the first time given at Cambridge in 1602. If so, the manuscript has unquestionably received additions during the four years before its appearance in print. The fact is, we find in the play certain evident allusions which could not possibly have been added before the years 1603-4; for instance, references to the translators of Montaigne--John Florio, and the friends who aided him;--references which must have been made after the Essais were published.
In act i. sc. 2, Judicio speaks of the English 'Flores Poetarum, against whom can-quaffing hucksters shoot their pellets.' These 'Flores *Poetarum' are* Florio and his fellow-workers, among whom Ben Jonson is also to be reckoned; and we shall see farther on that the

latter abuses these offensive hucksters as 'vernaculous orators,' because they make Montaigne the target of their sneers. Again, in act iv. sc. 2, Furor Poeticus, Ingenioso, and Phantasma indulge in expressions which can only apply to the Dedications and the Sonnets of Florio's translation. Phantasma, for instance, addresses an Ode of Horace to himself:--

'Maecenas, atavis edite regibus,
O et praesidium et dulce decus meum
Dii faciant votis vela secunda tuis.'

The latter line ought to run:--

Sunt, quos curriculo pulverem Olympicum,

and if we take into consideration that Juror says in the same scene:--

And when thy swelling vents amain,
Then Pisces be thy sporting chamberlain,

it is not asserting too much that these are manifest hits at Florio, who, to please his Maecenas, tries with Dr. Diodati, his 'guide-fish' to capture the 'whale' in the 'rocke rough ocean.' Florio's way of translating the Latin classic writers into indifferent English rhymes is also repeatedly ridiculed. The latter (Florio, p. 574.) once gives a passage from Plautus (The Captives, Prologue, v. 22) correctly enough: 'The Gods, perdye (pardieu), doe reckon and racket us men as their tennis balls.' Furor Poeticus, in one of his fits of fine frenzy, accuses Phoebus:--

The heavens' promoter that doth peep and prey
Into the acts of mortal tennis balls.

This he says after having, in the same highly comic speech, travestied Florio's Dedication of the third book, in which that gallant compares himself to 'Mercury between the radiant orbs of Venus and the Moon'--that is, the two ladies to whom he dedicates the book in question, and before whom he alleges he 'leads a dance.' A further sneer is directed by Furor Poeticus against the lazy manner with which Florio's Muse rises from her nest. Additional allusions to dramatic publications from the years 1603-4 will be found on pp. 201, 202. Another proof that the play (The Return from Parnassus) cannot be of a uniform cast, is this: In act i. sc. 2 a list of the poets is given, that are to be criticised. The list is kept up in proper succession as far as 'John Davis.' Then there are variations, and names not contained in that list. These additions mostly refer to dramatic authors, whilst the previous names, as far as 'John Davis,' only refer to lyric poets.

We believe the intention of the first writer of The Return from Parnassus was only to criticise lyric poets. Moreover, Monius says in the Prologue:--'What is presented here, is an old musty show, that has lain this twelvemonth in the bottom of a coal-house amongst brooms and old shoes.' Our opinion is that The Return from Parnassus, after having been acted before a learned public at Cambridge, came into the hands of players who applied the manner in which lyric poets had been criticised in it, to dramatic writers. The authors of the additions must have been friends of Shakspere; for, as we shall find, the enemies of the latter are also theirs.

2: Act iv. sc. 3.

3: In The Poetaster, of which we shall speak farther on.

4: According to certain indications in Satiromastix, he had an 'ambling' walk, or dancing kind of step. (See note 28.)

5: Collier's Memoirs of Alleyn, pp. 50 and 51.

6: Conversations with Drummond.

7: Satiromastix, 1602.

8: Collier's Drama, i. 334.

9: Poetaster.

10: Compare his Dedication in Volpone, of which we shall have more to say.

11: Drummond's Conversations.

12: Of all styles, Jonson liked best to be named 'Honest;' and he 'hath ane hundred letters so naming him.'-- Conversations with Drummond.

13: Life of Dryden, p. 265.

14: By Aubrey called 'Jack Young.'

15: As if the whole world had made it a point to conspire against Jonson, Gifford laboriously exerts himself to defend him against the numberless attacks of all the previous commentators, critics, and biographers. The endeavour of Gifford to whitewash him seems to me as fruitless a beginning as that of the little innocent represented in a picture as trying to change, with sponge and soap, the African colour of her nurse's face.

16: Jonson's Eulogy of Shakspere was composed seven years after the death of the latter. Having most probably been requested by Heminge and Condell not to withhold his tribute from the departed, to whom both his contemporaries as well as posterity had done homage, Jonson may readily have seized the occasion to do amends for the wrong he had inflicted upon the great poet during his lifetime. A later opinion of Jonson in regard to Shakspere (Timber; or Discoveries made upon Men and Matter, 1630-37) is of a more moderate tone, and on some points in contradiction to the words of praise contained in the published poem.

17: Poetaster, Apol. Dialogue.

18: This Prologue is not contained in the first edition (1598), but only in the second (1616). It may, therefore, have been written in the meantime. It is supposed that it was so in 1606. (See Shakspere's Century of Praise, 1879, pp. 118, 119.)

19: Only a few of the earliest productions of Jonson have come down to us. Some of them are: Every Man in His Humour (1598); Every Man out of His Humour (1599); and Cynthia's

Revels (1600), all of them full of personal allusions. Many of these are meant against Shakspere. We cannot, however, enter more fully upon that, as we have to confine ourselves to the chief controversy out of which Hamlet arose. Neither on Jonson's nor on Shakspere's part did the controversy cease after the appearance of Hamlet. It was still carried on through several dramas, which, however, we leave untouched, as not belonging to our theme.

20: See note 25.

21: In Satiromastix this reproach is made to Ben Jonson:--'Horace did not screw and wriggle himselfe into great Mens famyliarity, impudentlie as thou doost.'

22: Gifford, in his nervous anxiety to parry every reproach against his much-admired, and, in his eyes, blameless Jonson whose quarrelsomeness had from so many parts been properly charged, and particularly desirous of shielding him against the accusation of having taken up an attitude hostile to Shakspere, declares, in contradiction to the opinion of all previous commentators, that Crispinus is to represent John Marston. Since then, Gifford's assertion has been taken for granted, without deeper inquiry. The authority of this fond editor of Jonson has, however, proved an untrustworthy one in many things, especially in matters relating to Shakspere. Thanks to the exertions of more recent inquirers, not a a few things are now seen in a better perspective than Gifford was able to offer. We admit the difficulty of reconstructing facts from productions like The Poetaster, which had been dictated by the overwrought feelings of the moment. But in a satire which bred so much 'tumult,' which 'could so deeply offend,' and 'stir so many hornets' (four hundred persons out of five hundred being able to point with their fingers, in one instant, at one and the same man), the characters must have been very broadly drawn for general recognition. By such broad traits we must still be guided in our judgment to-day. All the characteristic qualities of Crispinus, which we shall explain farther on, prove that Gifford's idea about Crispinus being John Marston is not tenable.

This latter poet was very well versed in Greek and Latin, and had a complete classic education. The admonition of Horace to perfect himself in both languages, is therefore not applicable to him. Furthermore, Marston, at the time The Poetaster was composed (this may have been towards the end of the year 1600, or the beginning of 1601), had scarcely yet written anything for the stage. Only his Metamorphosis of Pigmalion's Image and Certaine Satyres (1598), and his Scourge of Villanie (1599) had been published. His first tragedy came out in print in 1602; it may just have been in course of becoming known on the stage. We have no means of ascertaining whether it had already been acted when The Poetaster appeared. This much is however certain, that when this latter satire obtained publicity, Marston's relations to the drama and the stage must yet have been of the most insignificant kind; for Philip Henslowe, in his Diary (pp. 156, 157), expressly speaks of him, even in 1599, as a 'new' poet to whom he had lent, through an intermediary, the sum of forty shillings 'in earneste of a Boocke,' the title of which is not mentioned. Is it, then, conceivable that such a dramatist who in 1601 certainly was yet very insignificant, should have been made the subject, in 1601, in Jonson's Poetaster, of the following very characteristic remark--assuming Crispinus to have been intended for Marston?

Tucca says, in regard to the former, to a poor player (act iii. sc. i):--'If he pen for thee once, thou shalt not need to travel with thy pumps full of gravel any more, after a blind jade and a hamper, and stalk upon boards and barrel-heads to an old cracked trumpet.'

Does this not quite fit Shakspere's popularity and dramatic success?

Jonson, it is true, tells Drummond that he had written his Poetaster against Marston. (According to his declaration in the

'Apologetical Dialogue,' there is nothing personal in the whole Poetaster! 'I can profess I never writt that piece more innocent or empty of offence.') However, we form our judgment in this matter from the clear, well-marked, and indubitably characteristic traits of the play, as well as from the results of modern criticism, which are fully in harmony with those traits. Everything points to the figure of Ovid being a mask for Marston. Jonson perhaps chose the name of Ovid for him because he, too, had written Metamorphoses. Besides the before-mentioned Metamorphosis of Pigmalion's Image, it is not improbable that Marston is the author of the manuscript preserved in the British Museum:--The New Metamorphosis; or, A Feaste or Fancie of Poeticall Legendes. The first parte divided into twelve books. Written by I. M., gent., 1600. Ovid--Marston--in the Poetaster, is described as the younger son of a gentleman of considerable position. He is dependent on a stipend allowed to him by his father. After having absolved his studies, he is to become an advocate, but secretly he devotes his time to poetry. The father warns him that poverty will be his lot if he does not renounce poetry. Ovid senior makes the following reproach to his son (which probably has reference to Marston's first tragedy, Antonio and Mellida):--'I hear of a tragedy of yours coming forth for the common players there, called Medea. By my household gods, if I come to the acting of it, I'll add one tragic part more than is yet expected to it.... What? shall I have my son a stager now? an enghle for players?... Publius, I will set thee on the funeral pile first!'

All this harmonises with the few facts we know of Marston's career, who is said to have been the son of a counsellor of the Middle Temple, who was at Corpus Christi College at Oxford, and who was made a baccalaureus there on February 23, 1592. In comparison with Crispinus and Demetrius, Ovid is but mildly chaffed; and this, again, is in accord with the relations which soon after arose, in a very friendly manner, between Jonson and Marston. It is scarcely to be thought that, if Marston had been derided as Crispinus, he would already have composed, as early as 1603, his eulogistic poem on Jonson's *Sejanus*, and dedicated to him in 1604, in such hearty words, his own *Malcontent*.

From some pointed words in the libel composed by Crispinus against Horace, Gifford concludes that the former must be Marston, because we meet with these pointed words in some satires and dramas of Marston. We, on our part, go, in these controversial plays, by the main and most prominent characteristics; and these show that Crispinus is Shakspere, and Ovid Marston.

The latter even once says (*Scourge of Villanie*, sat. vi.) that many a one, in reading his *Pigmalion*, has compared him to Ovid. In order to make out Crispinus to be guilty before Augustus, strong language is required. For this purpose, Jonson may have used the way and manners of Marston, and applied some of his newly coined graphic words. But this proves nothing for the identity of characters. The libel also contains a pointed word of Shakspere--'retrograde'--an expression little employed by the latter, and which is hurled as a reproach against Parolles, the figure which in all likelihood is to represent Jonson; Helena (act i. sc. 2) says to him, that he was born under Mars, 'when he was retrograde.'

The remark in The Return from Parnassus that few of the University can pen plays well, smelling too much of that writer Ovid and that writer *Metamorphosis*, has, in our opinion, also reference to John Marston whose first dramatic attempts--although he, like Jonson, may be called a 'University man'--do not admit of any comparison with those of Shakspere.

23: Demetrius repentingly admits that it was from envy he had ill-treated Horace, because 'he kept better company for the most part than I, better men loved him than loved me; and his writings thrived better than mine, and were better liked and graced.'

24: The little word 'clutcht' for a long time 'sticks strangely' in Crispinus' throat; it is only thrown up with the greatest difficulty.

In Hamlet (act v. sc. i, in the second verse of the grave-digger's song) we hear, 'Hath claw'd me in his clutch. In the original song, which is here travestied, the words are, 'Hath claw'd me with his crouch'.

25: The following allusion in The Poetaster (act iv. sc. 3) also has reference to Twelfth Night:--'I have read in a book that to play the fool wisely is high wisdom.' For Viola (act iii. sc. i) says:--

This fellow 's wise enough to play the fool;
And, to do that well, craves a kind of wit...
As full of labour as a wise man's art.

There are several indications in The Poetaster pointing to Shakspere's Julius Caesar which had appeared in the same year (1601). Not only does Horace say to Trebatius that 'great Caesar's wars cannot be fought with words,' but he also corrects Shakspere, who makes Antony (act iii. sc. 2) speak of Caesar's gardens on this side of the Tiber, by putting into the mouth of Horace (act iii. sc. i) the words:--' On the far side of all Tyber yonder.' In this scene, where the two Pyrgi are examined, there are some more allusions to Julius Caesar. Even the boy, whose instrument Brutus takes away when he is asleep, is not wanting. In The Poetaster it is a drum, instead of a lyre (the drum in All's Well that Ends Well). And are the following words of the same scene no satire upon act i. sc. 3 of Julius Caesar, where Casca and Cicero meet amidst thunder and lightning?

2 Pyrgi. Where art thou, boy? where is Calipolis?
Fight earthquakes in the entrails of the earth,
And eastern whirlwinds in the hellish shades;
Some foul contagion of the infected heavens
Blast all the trees, and in their cursed tops
The dismal night-raven and tragic owl
Breed and become forerunners of my fall!

Casca dwells especially on the 'bird of night.'

26: The y, in Pygmalion, seems to us not without cause to be changed by Marston into an i.

27: The number of metaphors used by Shakspere in 'Venus and Adonis,' which Marston travesties, is strikingly large.

28: A few instances may here be given of the coarseness with which Dekker pays back Jonson for his personal allusions. In The Poetaster, Crispinus is told that his 'satin-sleeve begins to fret at the rug that is underneath it.' In Satiromastix, Tucca cries out against Horace (Jonson):--'Thou never yet fel'st into the hands of sattin.' And again:--'Thou borrowedst a gowne of Roscius the stager, and sentest it home lousie.' Crispinus, in The Poetaster, is derided on account of his short legs. In Satiromastix, Horace is laughed at for his 'ambling' walk; wherefore he had so badly played mad Jeronimo's part. Jonson is reproached with all his sins: that he had killed a player; that he had not thought it necessary to keep his word to those whom he held to be heretics *and* infidels, and so forth. His face, which, as above mentioned, had scorbutic marks, is stated to be 'like a rotten russet apple when it is bruiz'd'; or, like the cover of a warming-pan, 'full of oylet-holes.' He is called an 'uglie Pope Bonifacius;' also a 'bricklayer;' and he is asked why, instead of building chimneys and laying down bricks, he makes 'nothing but railes'--'filthy rotten railes'--upon which alone his Muse leans. ('Railes' has a double meaning here: rails for fencing in a house; and gibes.) He is told that his feet stamp as if he had mortar under them--an allusion to his metrics, as well as to his ambling walk.

29: Shakspere was already then the proprietor of a house--New Place, in Stratford. In this scene Horace also asks Crispinus:--'You have much of the mother in you, sir? Your father is dead?' John Shakspere, the father, died in the year when The Poetaster was first performed--in September, 1601.

30: Twelfth Night, act iii. sc. 2. Sir Toby:--'Let there

be gall in thy ink, though thou write with a goose-pen.'

31: Here Crispinus threatens Horace with the 'purge' (a word that may be used as a noun or a verb), which, in The Return from Parnassus, is mentioned as having been administered by Shakspere to Jonson. It is highly probable that the reconciliation between Crispinus and Horace, which is described in the beginning of Satiromastix, had taken place between Shakspere and Ben Jonson, and that, during this period of peace, the performance of Sejanus occurred, in which Shakspere actively co-operated. After that, traces of hostility only are to be discovered between the two poets.
Even when Horace, in the 'Satiromastix,' has again broken the peace, the gentle Crispinus says to him:--
   Were thy warpt soule put in a new molde,
   I'd weare thee as a jewell set in golde.

32: The Satiromastix was performed in 1602, probably in the beginning of the year, as the Epilogue speaks of cold weather, and Dekker scarcely would have waited a year with his answer to The Poetaster. Queen Elizabeth died in 1603. Another decennium had to pass (Shakspere had long since withdrawn to his Stratford) before the taste of Whitehall had been so much lowered that Jonson could become a favourite of the courtly element.

33: In such type it is printed in the original.

34: In Satiromastix, Captain Tucca once bawls out against Horace, 'My name's Hamlet Revenge!' as if it had become known already then in the dramatic world that Shakspere was preparing his reply to The Poetaster. In the latter play (act iii. sc. I) which was probably added after The Poetaster had already been acted, and Jonson had heard that Dekker was writing his Satiromastix), Jonson makes a player from the other side of the Tiber say:--'We have hired him to abuse Horace, and bring him in, in a play, with all his gallants, as Tibullus, Mecaenas, Cornelius Gallus, and the rest....O, it will get us a huge deal of money, Captain, and we have need on't; for this winter has made us all poorer than so many starved snakes. Nobody comes at us, not a gentleman, nor a--'

In the same scene Tucca utters curses, before that player, against the theatres on the other side of the Tiber. The actor he addresses belongs to one of them. Tucca mentions two theatres by name--'your Globes, and your Triumphs.' He says to the actor:--'Commend me to seven shares and a half.' Shakespere and his colleagues had certain fixed shares in the 'Globe;' and the words of the actor, as regards the poor winter they had, confirm that which Shakspere gives to understand in Hamlet, that 'there was, for a while, no money bid for argument, unless the poet and the player went to cuffs in the question.'

VI.
'VOLPONE,' by Ben Jonson.

'EASTWARD HOE,' by Chapman, Ben Jonson, and Marston.

'THE MALCONTENT,' by John Marston.

Ben Jonson's 'Volpone' was first acted in 1605; and on February 11, 1607, it appeared in print. [1] It is preceded by a Dedication, in which the author dedicates 'both it and himself' to 'the most noble and most equal sisters, the two famous Universities,' in grateful acknowledgment 'for their love and acceptance shown to this Poem in the presentation.'

In this Dedication the most passionate language is used against all contemporary poets--especially against those who now, he says, practise 'in dramatic, as they term it: stage-poetry, nothing but ribaldry, profanation,' and 'all licence of offence to God and man.' Their petulancy, he continues, 'hath not only rapt me to present indignation, but made me studious heretofore;' for by them 'the filth of the time is uttered, and with such impropriety of phrase, such plenty of solecisms, such dearth of sense, so bold prolepses, so racked metaphors, with brothelry able to violate the ear of a pagan, and blasphemy to turn the blood of a Christian to water.'

Jonson expresses his purpose of standing off from them (the stage-poets) 'by all his actions.' Solemnly he utters this vow:--'I shall raise the despised head of poetry again, and, stripping her out of those rotten and base rags wherewith the times have adulterated her form, restore her to her primitive habit, feature, and majesty, and render her worthy to be embraced and kist of all the great and master-spirits of our world.' This object of his--he adds--'may most appear in this my latest work ('Volpone'), which you, most learned Arbitresses, have seen, judged, and, to my crown, approved; wherein I have laboured for their instruction and amendment, to reduce, not only the ancient forms, but manners of the scene, the easiness, the propriety, the innocence, and last, the doctrine, which is the principal end of poesie, to inform men in the best reason of living.'

All contemporary dramatists are most pitilessly condemned by Ben Jonson, and the cause of his present indignation is clearly stated: 'A name so full of authority, antiquity, and all great mark, is, through their insolence, become the lowest scorn of the age;' moreover, 'my (Jonson's) fame, and the reputation of divers honest and learned, are the question--that is to say, have been injured.

As in 'Volpone,' wherein Jonson, as he states, 'laboured for their (the contemporary poets') instruction and amendment,' we shall find most numerous allusions to Shakspere and 'Hamlet,' we feel justified in asserting that Jonson's whole fury is, in his 'present indignation,' roused against this particular author and against this special drama. Therein, as we have shown, a name of authority, antiquity, and all great mark--Montaigne--has been tampered with, and, through this satire, divers honest and learned (John Florio and his coadjutors in the translation--all friends of Jonson) have been injured, as well as the latter's own fame. In 'Hamlet,' Shakspere brought his own ideal of friendship in the figure of Horatio on the stage, in contrast to the Horace of 'The Poetaster.' Jonson was not the man to be edified by the beautiful examples and the nobler words of his gentle adversary, Shakspere, or to alter his sentiments in accordance with them. He rather welcomed every opportunity for a quarrel. That was the element in which he lived; for thus he got the materials and the spicy condiments for his dramas. Now in 'Hamlet' there were motives enough for lighting up a fire of hatred against Shakspere, and to entertain the public therewith.

Jonson, always ready for battle, willingly takes up the pen in their defence. In doing so, the favour of a nobleman and of some high-born ladies could be earned, at whose wish and request Montaigne had been Englished. Besides, every occasion was relished for opposing Shakspere, who had attacked Montaigne whose religious creed was the same as that of Jonson.

The British Museum possesses a copy of 'Volpone,' on which Jonson has, with his own hand, written the words:--'To his loving father and loving freind, Mr. John Florio, the ayde of his Muses: Ben Jonson seals this testemony of freindship and love.' Not the gift of this little book, however, but its contents--namely, the attack which Jonson made, both for the sake of his friend and for himself, against the great antagonist (Shakspere)--must be held to be the token or 'testemony of freindship and love.'

In the very beginning of the Dedication, Jonson says that every author ought to be heedful of his fame:--'Never, most equal sisters, had any man a wit so presently excellent as that it could raise itself, but there must come both matter, occasion, commenders, and favourers to it. If this be true, and that the fortune of all writers doth daily prove it, it behoves the careful to provide well towards these accidents; and, having acquired them, to preserve that part of reputation most tenderly, wherein the benefit of a friend is also defended.' He then asserts that this is an age in which poetry, and the professors of it, are so ill-spoken of on all sides because, in their petulancy, they have yet to learn that one cannot be a good poet without first being a good man.

In the following passage, curiously enough, a certain person is extolled as the model of a good man, against whom the stage dramatists, who themselves, according to Jonson, are not good men ('nothing remaining with them of the dignity of the poet'), have, as he thinks, grievously sinned:--' He that is said to be able to inform young men to all good disciplines, inflame grown men to all great virtues, keep old men in their best and supreme state, or, as they decline to childhood, recover them to their first strength; [2] that comes forth the interpreter and arbiter of nature, a teacher of things divine no less than human, [3] a master in manners; and can alone, or with a few, effect the business of mankind: [4] this, I take him, is no subject for pride and ance to exercise their railing rhetoric upon.'

In this description we again see Montaigne, against whom 'railing rhetoric' has been used.

Ben Jonson proudly points to himself as having never done such mischief: 'For my particular, I can, and from a most clear conscience, affirm that I have ever trembled to think toward the least profaneness.' Though--he says--he cannot wholly escape 'from some the imputation of sharpness,' he does not feel guilty of having offered insult to anyone, 'except to a mimic, cheater, bawd, or buffoon.' But--'I would ask of these supercilious politics, what nation, society, or general order of state I have provoked? ... What public person? Whether I have not, in all these, preserved their dignity, as mine own person, safe? ... Where have I been particular? where personal?'

Who does not see in the following words a reproach launched against Shakspere, that he has taken his materials from other writers? Who does not feel that the warning addressed to 'wise and noble persons' has reference to the highly placed protectors of the great rival whose favour Ben Jonson, in spite of his Latin and Greek, was not able to obtain? He says:--

'Application' (that is, plagiarism) 'is now grown a trade with many; and there are that profess to have a key for the decyphering of everything: but let wise and noble persons take heed how they be too credulous, or give leave to these invading interpreters to be over-familiar with their fames, who cunningly, and often, utter their own virulent malice under other men's simplest meanings.'

Jonson then approves of those 'severe and wise patriots' who, in order to provide against 'the hurts these licentious spirits may do in a State,' rather desire to see plays full of 'fools and devils,' and 'those antique relics of barbarism' (he means 'Masques,' which he wrote with great virtuosoship) acted on the stage, than 'behold the wounds of private men, of princes and nations.'

And now we come to the passage, partly already quoted, which more than anything else shows that the 'purge' which 'our fellow Shakspere gave him'--'Hamlet'--must have greatly damaged, in the eyes of the public, both the reputation of Jonson and of his friends. He confesses it in these remarkable words:--

'I cannot but be serious in a cause of this nature, wherein my fame, and the reputation of divers honest and learned are the question; when a name so full of authority, antiquity, and all great mark, is, through their insolence, become the lowest scorn of the age; and those men subject to the petulancy of every vernaculous orator, that were wont to be the care of kings and happiest monarchs.' [5]

Is there a character, we may ask, not only in Shakspere's dramas, but in any play of that period, to which the description given by Jonson could apply?--of course, Hamlet always excepted, who is but a mask for Montaigne. And who else but Montaigne is designated by the expressions: 'a name so full of authority, antiquity, and all great mark;' 'the care of kings and happiest monarchs?'

That the 'railing rhetoric' in which such a character was derided, could not be contained in a satirical poem, but had reference to a drama, is proved, as already explained, by the fact of Jonson's wrath being directed against the stage-poets. He says expressly, that henceforth, by all his actions, he will 'stand off from them.' To the most learned authorities, the two Universities, he announces that, by his own regular art, he intends giving these wayward disciples of Dramatic Poesy proper instruction and amendment. Had his object not been to strike the most popular of the stage-poets--Shakspere--he would have been bound to make an exception for that name of which everyone must have thought first when stage-poets were subjected to reproof. We repeat: Jonson only intended measuring himself against him who was the greatest of his time. This was fully in accordance with his disputatious inclination. [6]

The person once 'wont to be the care of kings and happiest monarchs' [7] must have been a foreigner, for we do not know of any favourite 'full of authority and antiquity' who enjoyed such high privilege from English kings. However, if a dramatist had been bold enough to put such a favourite on the stage, he would have met with the most severe punishment long before Jonson had pointed out his reprehensible audacity. By the 'happiest monarchs,' Henry III. and Henry IV. of France are meant. The latter, at that time, yet stood in the zenith of his good fortune. Again, the expression: 'of every vernaculous orator,' points to the circumstance of the mockery being directed against a foreigner; and the same may be said of Jonson's question, addressed to supercilious politicians, as to what nation, society, or general order of State he had provoked? Clearly, another nation, a society of different modes of thought than the English one, and foreign institutions, are here indicated.

We now come to some hints contained in 'Volpone,' which partly consist of an endeavour to expose Shakspere on account of plagiarisms committed against other writers, partly of references to irreligious tendencies, against which Jonson warns, and which he strives to ridicule.

Under the existing strict laws which forbade religious questions being discussed on the stage, the latter references had to be made in parable manner, but still not too covertly, so that they might be understood by a certain audience--namely, the members of the Universities of Oxford and Cambridge. [8]

Already, in the Prologue of his 'Volpone,' Jonson says of himself that--

In all his poems still hath been this measure,
To mix profit with your pleasure.

He also despises certain deceptive tricks of composition:--

Nor hales he in a gull old ends reciting,
To stop gaps in his loose writing;
With such a deal of monstrous and forced action,
As might make Bethlem a faction:
Nor made he his play for jests stolen from each table,
But makes jests to fit his fable....
The laws of time, place, persons he observeth,
From no needful rule he swerveth.

In the observance of the technical rules of the classic drama--this much Jonson could certainly prove to the world--he was superior to Shakspere. The severe words: 'monstrous and forced action,' can only refer to a drama written not long before; for, in 'Volpone,' Jonson wishes to give to the stage-poets of his time his own ideal of a drama. 'Bethlem' (Bedlam) indicates madness round which all kinds of lunatics might gather as factionaries or adherents of the kind of drama which Jonson wishes to stigmatise.

Do we go too far in thinking that 'Hamlet' is the play which is made the target of allusions in this very Prologue?

However, we proceed at once to the Interlude which follows after the first scene of the first act of 'Volpone.' In it, Shakspere himself is practically put on the stage, by being asked:

> how of late thou hast suffered translation,
> And shifted thy coat in these days of reformation.

This Interlude is in no connection with the course of the dramatic action.

Mosca, a parasite, brings in, for the entertainment of his master (Volpone), three merry Jack Andrews. One of them, Androgyno, must be held to be SHAKSPERE.

Here we have to note that Francis Meres, a scholar of great repute, and M.A. of both Universities, wrote in 1598 a book, entitled 'Palladis Tamia,' which in English he calls 'Wit's Treasury.' It contains, so far as the sixteenth century is concerned, the most valuable statements as regards Shakspere: nay, the only trustworthy ones dating from that century. In that work, Meres classifies and criticises the poets of his time and country by comparing each of them with some Greek or Roman poet, kindred to the corresponding English one in the line of production chosen and in quality. Ben Jonson is only mentioned once, at a very modest place; his name stands last, after Chapman and Dekker.

Meres confers upon Shakspere most enthusiastic but just praise:--

'As the soule of Euphorbus was thought to live in Pythagoras: so the sweete, wittie soul of Ovid lives in mellifluous and hony-tongued Shakespeare; witness his 'Venus and Adonis;' his 'Lucrece;' his sugred 'Sonnets' among his private friends.... As Plautus and Seneca are accounted the best for Comedy and Tragedy amongst the Latines: so Shakspere among the English is the most excellent in both kinds for the stage.'

He then mentions twelve of his plays, [9] and thus concludes his eulogy:--

'As Epius Stolo said that the Muses would speake with Plautus tongue, if they would speak Latin: so I say that the Muses would speak with Shakespeare's fine filed phrases if they would speake English.'

The envious Jonson who pledges himself, in the Dedication to the two Universities, to give back to Poesy its former majesty, may have considered it necessary, before all, to deride, before a learned audience, the enthusiastic praise conferred by Francis Meres upon Shakspere, as well as Shakspere himself on account of the free religious tendencies he had expressed in 'Hamlet' This is done, as we said, in the Interlude prepared by Mosca for the entertainment of his master. Volpone boasts of the clever manner with which he gains riches:--

> I use no trade, no venture;
> I wound no earth with ploughshares, fat no beasts
> To feed the shambles; have no mills for iron,
> Oil, corn, or men, to grind them into powder:
> ... expose no ships
> To threatenings of the furrow-faced sea;

I turn no monies in the public bank,
Nor usure private.

Mosca, in order to flatter his master, continues the speech of the latter in the same strain:--

... No, sir, nor devour
Soft prodigals. You shall have some will swallow
A melting heir as glibly as your Dutch
Will pills of butter, and ne'er purge for it; [10]
Tear forth the fathers of poor families
Out of their beds, and coffin them alive
In some kind clasping prison, where their bones
May be forthcoming, when the flesh is rotten:
But your sweet nature doth abhor these courses;
You lothe the widow's or the orphan's tears
Should wash your pavements, or their piteous cries
Ring in the roofs, and beat the air for vengeance.

We have here an allusion to Hamlet, [11] where he asks the Ghost why the sepulchre has opened its 'ponderous and marble jaws' to cast him up again; also to the Queen and whilom widow; and, furthermore, to the orphans, Ophelia and Laertes, and to the tears shed by the latter at his sister's death. The cry of vengeance refers to the similar utterances of the Ghost, of Hamlet, and of Laertes, who all seek revenge.

Mosca, with a view of preparing for his master a pleasure more suitable to his taste than that which a play like 'Hamlet,' we suppose, could afford him, brings in the three gamesters:--Nano, a dwarf; Castrone, a eunuch; and Androgyne, a hermaphrodite. [12] The latter is meant to represent Shakspere; for he is introduced by Nano as a soul coming from Apollo, which migrated through Euphorbus and Pythagoras (Meres uses these two names in his eulogy of the soul of Shakspere). [13]

After having recounted several other stages in the migration of Androgyne's soul (we shall mention them further on), the latter has to give an answer why he has 'shifted his coat in these days of reformation,' and why his 'dogmatical silence' has left him. He replies that an obstreperous 'Sir Lawyer' had induced him to do so. From this it may be concluded that Bacon had some influence on Shakspere's 'Hamlet.' Are not, in poetical manner, the same principles advocated in 'Hamlet,' which Bacon promoted in science? [14]

After the Hermaphrodite has admitted that he has become 'a good dull mule,' [15] he avows that he is now a very strange beast, an ass, an actor, a hermaphrodite, and a fool; and that he more especially relishes this latter condition of his, for in all other forms, as Jonson makes him confess, he has 'proved most distressed.' [16]

Let us now quote from this Interlude some highly-spiced satirical passages.

Nano, the dwarf, coming in with Androgyno and Castrone, asks for room for the new gamesters or players, and says to the public:--

> They do bring you neither play, nor university show;
> And therefore do intreat you that whatsoever they rehearse,
> May not fare a whit the worse, for the false pace of the verse. [17]
> If you wonder at this, you will wonder more ere we pass,
> For know, here [18] is inclosed the soul of Pythagoras, [19]
> That juggler divine, as hereafter shall follow;
> Which soul, fast and loose, sir, came first from Apollo.

It is explained how that soul afterwards transmigrated into 'the goldy-locked Euphorbus who was killed, in good fashion, at the siege of old Troy, by the cuckold of Sparta;' how it then passed into Hermotimus, 'where no sooner it was missing, but with one Pyrrhus of Delos [20] it learned to go a-fishing;' [21] how thence it did enter the Sophist of Greece, Pythagoras. After having been changed into whom,

> she became a philosopher,
> Crates the cynick, as itself doth relate it: [22]
> Since kings, knights and beggars, knaves, lords, and fools get it,
> Besides ox and ass, camel, mule, goat, and brock, [23]
> In all which it has spoke, as in the cobbler's cock. [24]

Nano's present intention, however, is not to refer to such things:--

> But I come not here to discourse of that matter,
> Or his one, two, or three, or his great oath, BY QUATER, [25]
> His musics,[26] his trigon, his golden thigh, [27]
> Or his telling how elements [28] shift: but I
> Would ask, how of late thou hast suffered translation
> And shifted thy coat in these days of Reformation.

Androgyno. Like one of the reformed, a fool, as you see, COUNTING ALL OLD DOCTRINE HERESIE.

Nano. But not on thine own forbid meats hast thou ventured.

Androgyno. On fish, when first a Carthusian I entered.[29]

Nano. Why, then thy dogmatical silence hath left thee?

Androgyno. Of that an obstreperous lawyer bereft me.

Nano. O wonderful change, when sir lawyer forsook thee!
For Pythagore's sake, what body then took thee?

Androgyno. A good dull mule.

Nano. And how! by that means Thou wert brought to allow of
the eating of beans?

Androgyno. Yes.

Nano. But from the mule into whom didst thou pass?

Androgyno. Into a very strange beast, by some writers called
an ass;
By others, a precise, pure, illuminate brother,
Of those devour flesh, and sometimes one another;
And will drop you forth a libel, or a sanctified lie,
Betwixt every spoonful of a Nativity [30] pie.

Nano then admonishes Androgyno to quit that profane nation. Androgyno answers that he gladly remains in the shape of a fool and a hermaphrodite. To the question of Nano, as to whether he likes remaining a hermaphrodite in order to 'vary the delight of each sex,' Androgyno replies:--

Alas, those pleasures be stale and forsaken;
No 't is your fool wherewith I am so taken,
The only one creature that I can called blessed;
For all other forms I have proved most distressed.

Nano. Spoke true, as thou wert in Pythagoras still.
This learned opinion we celebrate will,...

With a song, praising fools, the Interlude closes.

In act ii. sc. 2, after Mosca and Volpone have erected a stage upon the stage, Volpone enters, disguised as a mountebank, and abuses those 'ground ciarlatani' (charlatans, impostors) 'who come in lamely, with their mouldy tales out of Boccaccio.' Then there is a most clear allusion to Hamlet (act iv. sc. 6), where he informs his friend Horatio, by letter, of his voyage to England when he was made prisoner by pirates, who dealt with him 'like thieves of mercy.' A further remark of Volpone on 'base pilferies,' and 'wholesome penance done for it,' may be taken as a hit against Hamlet's 'fingering' the packet to 'unseal their grand commission;' for which, in Jonson's view, he would be forced by his father confessor, in a well-regulated Roman Catholic State, to do penance.

This is what Volpone says:--

'No, no, worthy gentlemen; to tell you true, I cannot endure to see the rabble of these ground ciarlatani, that ... come in lamely, with their mouldy tales out of Boccaccio, like stale Tabarine, the fabulist; some of them discoursing their travels; and of their tedious captivity [31] in the Turks' galleys, when, indeed, were the truth known, they were the Christians' gallies, where very temperately they eat bread and drunk water, as a wholesome penance, [32] enjoined them by their confessors for base pilferies.'

Shakspere, as we have already explained, got a 'pill' in 'The Poetaster,' whereupon 'our fellow Shakespeare,' as is maintained in the 'Return from Parnassus,' 'has given him' (Jonson) 'a purge that made him bewray his credit' Now Ben, clearly enough, calls this answer of the great adversary--a 'finely wrapt-up antimony,' whereby minds 'stopped with earthy oppilations,' are purged into another world.

Volpone says:--'These turdy-facy, nasty-paty, lousy-fartical rogues, with one poor groat's worth of unprepared antimony, finely wrapt up in several scartoccios (covers), [33] are able, very well, to kill their twenty a week, and play; yet these meagre, starved spirits, who have stopt the organs of their minds with earthy oppilations, want not their favourers among your shrivelled sallad-eating artizans, [34] who are overjoyed that they may have their half-pe'rth of physic; though it purge them into another world, it makes no matter.'

Jonson then continues his satire against 'Hamlet' by making Volpone, disguised as a mountebank, sell medicine which is to render that 'purge' ('Hamlet') perfectly innocuous. He calls his medicine 'Oglio del Scoto:' [35] good for strengthening the nerves; a sovereign remedy against all kinds of illnesses; and, 'it stops a dysenteria, immediately.'

Nano praises its miraculous effects in a song:--

> Had old Hippocrates, or Galen,
> That to their books put med'cines all in,
> But known this secret, they had never
> (Of which they will be guilty ever)
> Been murderers of so much paper,
> Or wasted many a hurtless taper;
> No Indian drug had e'er been famed,
> Tobacco, sassafras not named;
> Ne yet of guacum one small stick, sir,
> Nor Raymund Lully's great elixir.
> Ne had been known the Danish Gonswart,
> Or Paracelsus, with his long sword.

Is not HAMLET here as good as indicated by name?

The Danish Prince appears on the stage in his 'inky cloak.' No doubt, Jonson picked up the word 'Gonswart' (gansch-zwart, in Flemish) among his Flemish, Dutch, and other Nether-German comrades of war in the Low Countries. Surely, the Danish Prince 'All-Black' is none else but Hamlet clad in black.

In the same scene, the connection between Hamlet and Ophelia also is satirically pulled to pieces. In 'Eastward Hoe' (1605), Jonson and his party do the same in the most indecent and most despicable manner.

Nano, praising the sublime virtues of the 'Oglio del Scoto,' sings:--

Would you live free from all diseases?
Do the act your mistress pleases,
Yet fright all aches from your bones?
Here's a medicine for the nones. [36]

The scene of the action in 'Volpone' is laid in Venice. During the whole scene above-mentioned, Sir Politick Would-Be and a youthful gentleman-traveller are present Others have already pointed out that, by the former, Shakspere is meant. [37] The traveller, Peregrine, is a youth whom the jealous Lady Politick once declares to be 'a female devil in a male outside,'--again an allusion to Shakspere's 'two loves' which he himself describes in Sonnet 144.

The words, also, with which Hamlet (act iii. sc. 3) praises his friend Horatio (the Shaksperian ideal of a Horace) are ridiculed by Jonson in this scene. Sir Politick Would-Be says to Peregrine:--

Well, if I could but find one man, one man,
To mine own heart, whom I durst trust, I would--

When the stage is raised on the theatre for Volpone, who is disguised as a quacksalver, Sir Politick wishes to enlighten Peregrine as to the fellows that 'mount the bank.' [38] We need not explain that this is directed against the 'so-called stage-poets' and players. It will easily be perceived that the meaning of the subsequent conversation is the same as in the Preface of 'Volpone,' where Jonson says that 'wis and noble persons 'ought to' take heed how they be too credulous, or give leave to these invading interpreters to be over-familiar with their fames.'

Sir Politick (describing the fellows, one of which is to mount the bank) says:--

> They are the only knowing men of Europe!
> Great general scholars, excellent physicians, [39]
> Most admired statesmen, profest favourites,
> And Cabinet counsellors to the greatest princes;
> The only languaged men of all the world!
>
> Peregrine. And I have heard, they are most lewd [40] impostors
> Made all of terms and shreds, no less beliers
> Of great men's favours, than their own vile med'cines...

In act iv. sc. 1, Sir Politick gives counsels to the young Peregrine, which are a manifest satire upon Polonius' fatherly farewell speech to Laertes; and here again, let it be observed, religious tendencies are made the subject of persiflage.

> Sir Politick. First, for your garb, it must
> be grave and serious
> Very reserved and locked; not tell a secret
> On any terms, not to your father; scarce
> A fable, but with caution; make sure choice
> Both of your company and your discourse; beware
> You never speak a truth--....
> And then, for your religion, profess none,
> But wonder at the diversity of all;
> And, for your part, protest, were there no other
> But simply the laws o' th' land, you could content you.

Nic Machiavel and Monsieur Bodin, both
Were of this mind.

In act iii. sc. 2, it is openly said that English authors namely, such as understand Italian, have stolen from Pastor Fido 'almost as much as from MONTAIGNIE' (Montaigne). In vain we have looked for traces of Montaigne's Essays in other dramas that have come down to us from that epoch. That Shakspere must have been conversant with the Italian tongue, Charles Armitage Brown has tried to prove, and according to our opinion he has done so successfully. [41]

The talkative Lady Politick wishes to offer some distraction to the apparently sick Volpone. She recommends him an Italian book in these words:--

All our English writers,
I mean such as are happy in the Italian,
Will deign to steal out of this author mainly;
Almost as much as from Montagnie: [42]
He has so modern and facile a vein,
Fitting the time, and catching the court-ear! [43]

When Sir Politick (act v. sc. 2) is to be arrested (he is suspected of having got up a conspiracy, and betrayed the Republic of Venice to the Turks), he asserts his innocence; and when his papers are to be examined, he exclaims:--

Alas, Sir! I have none but notes
Drawn out of play-books--
And some essays. [44]

Mosca (act i-v. sc. 2), spurring on his counsel, says:--

Mercury sit upon your thundering tongue,
Or the French Hercules [45] and make your language
As conquering as his club, to beat along,
As with a tempest, flat, our adversaries.

Hamlet, when asked by the King how he 'calls the play, answers:--'The Mouse-trap.' Mosca calls his own cunningness with which he thinks he can overreach his master, the 'Fox-trap.'

If our intention were not to restrict this treatise to desirable limits, many more satirical passages might be pointed out in 'Volpone,' which are manifestly directed against 'Hamlet' and Shakspere. Those who take a deeper interest in the subject, will discover not a few passages of this kind in 'Volpone.'

In 1605--we believe, a few months before 'Volpone' [46]--'Eastward Hoe' came out, a comedy written by Ben Jonson, Chapman, and Marston, in which,
as already stated, the connection between Hamlet and Ophelia is derided in a low, burlesque manner.

Shakspere, in order to flagellate Montaigne's mean views about womankind, puts into the mouth of Ophelia, when she has no longer the control of her tongue, the hideous words:--'Come, my coach!' and 'Oh, how the wheel become it!' [47] This is a satirical hit, rapidly indicated, but only understood by those who had carefully read Montaigne's book. Ben Jonson, Chapman, and Marston try to make capital out of these expressions, by deriding and denouncing them to the crowd, in order to defame Shakspere.

Girtred (Gertrud, name of Hamlet's mother, the Queen,) is the figure under which Ophelia is ridiculed in 'Eastward Hoe.' [48] The first is a girl of loosest manners. Her ambition torments her to marry a nobleman, in order to obtain a 'coach.' To her mother (Mrs. Touchstone) she incessantly speaks words of most shameless indecency, which cannot be repeated; more especially as regards her 'coach,' for which she asks ever and anon. A lackey, called Hamlet, must procure it to her. We will give some fragments of that scene. The remainder cannot be offered to a modern circle of general readers.

Enter **Hamlet,** a Foote-man, in haste.

Hamlet. What coachman--my ladye's coach! for shame! Her ladiship's readie to come down.

Enter **Potkinne,** a Tankard-bearer.

Potkinne. 'Sfoote! Hamlet, are you madde? Whither run you nowe? You should brushe up my olde mistresse!

Thereupon neighbours come together, all impelled by the greatest curiosity 'to see her take coach,' and wishing to congratulate her.

Gertrud. Thank you, good people! My coach for the love of Heaven, my coach! In good truth, I shall swoune else.

Hamlet. Coach, coach, my ladye's coach! [Exit Hamlet.

After a little conversation between mother and daughter, which we must leave out, Hamlet enters again:

Hamlet. Your coach is coming, madam.

Gertrud. That's well said. Now Heaven! methinks I am eene up to the knees in preferment....
But a little higher, but a little higher, but a little higher!

There, there, there lyes Cupid's fire!

Mrs. Touchstone. But must this young man (Hamlet), an't please you, madam, run by your coach all the way a foote?

Gertrud. I by my faith, I warrant him; hee gives no other milke, as I have another servant does.

Mrs. Touchstone. Ahlas! 'tis eene pittie meethinks; for God's sake, madam, buy him but a hobbie horse; let the poore youth have something betwixt his legges to ease 'hem. Alas! we must doe as we would be done too.

That is all we dare to quote from this comedy; but it quite suffices to characterise the meanness of the warfare which Jonson's clique carried on against Shakspere.

However, the lofty ideas contained in 'Hamlet' could not be lowered by such an attack; they became the common property of the best and noblest. Those ideas were of too high a range, too abstract in their nature, to be easily made a sport of before the multitude. A few pleasantries, used by Shakespeare in a moment of easy-going style, were laid hold of maliciously, and caricatured most indecently, by his antagonists, in order to entertain the common crowd there with. Innocent children, moreover, were made to act such satires: 'little eyases, that cry out on the top of the question, and are most tyrannically clapped for't: these are now the fashion, and so berattle the common stages.'

Not less than in 'Volpone,' the tendency of 'Hamlet' as regards religious questions is, in the most evident manner, ridiculed in John Marston's 'Malcontent.' Although this satire (so the play is called in the preface 'To the Reader') appeared before 'Volpone,' we yet thought it more useful first to speak of Jonson's comedy being the work of

Shakspere's most formidable adversary.

'The Malcontent' was printed in 1604; and soon afterwards (in the same year) a second edition appeared, augmented by the author, as well as enriched by a few additions from the pen of John Webster. [49] The play is preceded by a Latin Dedication to Ben Jonson, which sufficiently shows that a close friendship must have existed, at that time, between the two. [50] The satire is replete with phrases taken from 'Hamlet' for the purpose of mockery; and they are introduced in the loosest, most disconnected manner, thus doubly showing the intention and purpose. Marston's style is pointedly described in 'The Return from Parnassus;' and we do not hesitate to say that the following criticism was written in consequence of his 'Malcontent:'--

> Methinks he is a ruffian in his style,
> Withouten bands or garters' ornament:
> He quaffs a cup of Frenchman's [51] Helicon,
> Then roister doister in his oily terms,
> Cuts, thrusts, and foins at whomsoever he meets...
> Tut, what cares he for modest close-couch'd terms,
> Cleanly to gird our looser libertines?...
> Ay, there is one, that backs a paper steed,
> And manageth a penknife gallantly,
> Strikes his poinardo at a button's breadth,
> Brings the great battering-ram of terms to towns;
> And, at first volley of his cannon-shot,
> Batters the walls of the old fusty world.

Who else can be indicated by the 'One' but Shakspere? To Marston's hollow creations, which drag the loftiest ideas through the mire to amuse the vulgar, the sublime and serious discourses of Shakspere are opposed, which are destined to afford profoundest instruction. Is not the whole tendency of 'Hamlet' described in the last two lines just quoted, in which it is stated that under this poet's attack the walls of the old fusty world are battered down? [52]

The chief character in 'The Malcontent' is a Duke of Genoa. Marston, in his preface 'To the Reader,' lays stress on the fact of this Duke being, not an historical personage, but a creation of fiction, so 'that even strangers, in whose State I laid my scene, should not from thence draw any disgrace to any, dead or living.' After having complained that, in spite of this endeavour of his, there are some who have been 'most unadvisedly over-cunning in misinterpreting' him, and, 'with subtletie, have maliciously spread ill rumours,' he goes on declaring that he desires 'to satisfie every firme spirit, who in all his actions proposeth to himself no more ends then God and vertue do, whose intentions are alwaies simple.' Those only he means to combat 'whose unquiet studies labor innovation, contempt of holy policie, reverent comely superioritie and establisht unity.' He fears not for the rest of his 'supposed tartnesse; but unto every worthy minde it will be approved so generall and honest as may modestly passe with the freedome of a satyre.'

That this satire could only be directed against 'Hamlet,' every one will be convinced who spends a short hour in reading Marston's 'Malcontent.' Here, too, we must confine ourselves to pointing out only the most important allusions; especially such as refer to religion. Indeed, we would have to copy the whole play, in order to make it fully clear how much Marston, with his undoubted talent for travesty, has succeeded in grotesquely deriding the lofty, noble tone of Shakspere's drama.

The chief character in 'The Malcontent' is Malevole, the Duke of Genoa before-mentioned, who has been wrongfully deprived of the crown. With subtle dissimulation, disguised and unknown, he hangs about the Court. Against the ladies especially, whom he

Shakspere And Montaigne

all holds to be adulteresses, he entertains the greatest mistrust. He watches every one; but most closely women. He is the image of mental distemper; and Pietro, the ruling Duke, describes him in act i. sc. 2 by saying that 'the elements struggle within him; his own soule is at variance within her selfe;' he is 'more discontent than Lucifer.' In short, he confers upon him all the qualities of a 'Hamlet' character.

Whenever religious questions are addressed to Malevole, we have to look upon him as the very type of Shakspere himself, whom Marston takes to task for his spirit of 'innovation' and his 'contempt of holy policie and establisht unity.' Shakspere, it ought to be remembered, had scourged Ben Jonson under the figure of Malvolio. Marston, who dedicates 'The Malcontent' to Jonson, no doubt wished to please Jonson by calling the chief character, which represents Shakspere, Malevole.

The play opens with an abominable charivari. ('The vilest out-of-time musicke being heard.') This is partly a hit against the Globe Theatre where--as we see from Shakspere's dramas--music was often introduced in a play; partly it is to indicate the disharmony of Malevole's mind.

Only a few travesties may be mentioned here, before we quote the treatment of religious questions.

In act i. sc. 7 (here the scene is ridiculed in which Hamlet, with drawn sword, stands behind the King), Pietro enters, 'his sword drawne.'

  Pietro. A mischiefe fill thy throate, thou fowle-jaw'd slave! Say thy praiers!

  Mendozo. I ha forgot um.

Pietro. Thou shall die.

Mendozo. So shall Ihou. I am heart-mad.

Pietro. I am horne-mad.

Mendozo. Extreme mad.

Pietro. Monstrously mad.

Mendozo. Why?

Pietro. Why? thou, thou hast dishonoured my bed.

Hamlet's words: [53]--'O, most wicked speed, to post with such dexterity to incestuous sheets!' are so often ridiculed because Shakspere, instead of the word 'bed,' uses the more unusual 'sheets.'

Aurelia [54] speaks of 'chaste sheets,' Malevole [55] prophesies that 'the Dutches (Duke, Doge) sheets will smoke for't ere it be long.' Mendozo [56] 'hates all women, waxe-lightes, antique bed-postes,' &c.; 'also sweete sheetes.' Aurelia, parodying the words Hamlet addresses to his mother, asks herself: 'O, judgement, where have been my eyes? What bewitched election made me dote on thee? what sorcery made me love thee?'

The counsel which Hamlet gives to his mother 'to throw away the worser part of her cleft heart,' Pietro ridicules in act i. sc. 7:--

My bosome and my heart,
When nothing helps, cut off the rotten part.

The splendid speech of Hamlet: 'What a piece of work is man!' sounds from Mendozo's [57] lips thus:--'In body how delicate; in soule how wittie; in discourse how pregnant; in life how warie; in favours how juditious; in day how sociable; in night how!--O pleasure unutterable!'

Hamlet's little monologue: [58] 'Tis now the very witching time of night,' runs thus with Mendozo:--[59]

'Tis now about the immodest waste of night;
The mother of moist dew with pallide light
Spreads gloomie shades about the mummed earth.
Sleepe, sleepe, whilst we contrive our mischiefes birth.

Then, parodying Hamlet as he draws forth the dead Polonius from behind the arras, Mendozo says:--

This man Ile (I'll) get inhumde.

Thus, all kinds of Shaksperian incidents and locutions are brought forward, wherever they are apt to produce the most comic effect. Several times, from the beginning, the 'weasel' is mentioned with which Hamlet rallies Polonius. We also hear of the 'sponge which sucks'--a simile used by Hamlet (act iv. sc. 3) in regard to Rosencrantz. Nor is the 'true-penny' forgotten--a word used by Hamlet [60] to designate his father's ghost as a true and genuine one; nor the 'Hillo, ho, ho.'

In all these allusions, of which an attentive reader might easily find scores, there is no systematic order of thoughts. Only in the religious questions we meet with a clear system: they are all addressed to Malevole, who is represented as a kind of freethinker, similar to the one whom Marston, in his preface, wishes to be outlawed, and of whom he says that he fully merits the 'tartness' and freedom of his satire. In the very beginning of 'The Malcontent,' Pietro asks Malevole:

I wonder what religion thou art of?

Malevole. Of a souldiers religion. [61]

Pietro. And what doost thinke makes most infidells now?

Malevole. Sects. Sects! I have seene seeming Pietie change her roabe so oft, that sure none but some arch-divell can shape her pitticoate.

Pietro. O! a religious pllicie.

Malevole. But damnation on a politique religion!

In act ii. sc. 5 we find the following:--

Malevole. I meane turne pure Rochelchurchman. [62]
I--

Mendozo. Thou Churchman! Why? Why?

Malevole. Because He live lazily, raile upon authoritie, deny Kings supremacy in things indifferent, and be a pope in mine owne parish.

Mendozo. Wherefore doost thou thinke churches were made?

Malevole. To scowre plow-shares. I have seene oxen plow uppe altares: Et nunc seges ubi Sion fuit.

Then there is again what appears to be an allusion to Hamlet, act i. sc. 4, resembling that in 'Volpone':--

I have seen the stoned coffins of long-flead Christians burst up and made hogs troughs.

In act iv. sc. 4, Mendozo says to Malevole, whom he wishes to use for the murder of a hermit:--

Yea, provident. Beware an hypocrite!
A Church-man once corrupted, Oh avoide!
A fellow that makes religion his stawking horse.
He breeds a plague. Thou shalt poison him.

From the many hints in 'Volpone' and in 'The Malcontent,' it clearly follows that Shakspere was to be represented, in those dramas, before the public at large, as an Atheist. [63] According to Jonson, he counted 'ALL OLD DOCTRINE HERESIE.' According to Marston, he had an aversion for all sects, and 'CONTEMPT OF HOLY POLICIE, REVERENT COMELY SUPERIORITIE, AND ESTABLISHT UNITIE.' We hope we
have convinced our readers that Shakspere spoke in matters of religion as clearly as his 'tongue-tied muse' [64] permitted him to do. Above all, we think of having successfully proved that the controversy of 'Hamlet' is directed against doctrines which assert that there is nothing but evil in human nature.

Shakspere's prophetic glance saw the pernicious character of Montaigne's inconsistent thoughts, which, unable to place us in sound relation to the Universe, only succeed in making men pass their lives in subtle reflection and unmanly, sentimental inaction. Shakspere, intending to avert the blighting influence of such a philosophy from the best and foremost of his country, wrote his 'Hamlet.' As a truly heaven-born poet he bound for ever, by Thought's enduring chain,

> All that flows unfixed and undefined
> In glimmering phantasy before the mind.

In spite of the powerful impression his master-work, 'Hamlet,' has made upon all thinking minds, the deepest and most serious meaning of Shakspere's warning words could not have been fathomed by the many. The parables through which a Prophet spoke were cast into the form of a theatrical play, not easy to understand for the mass of men; for 'tongue-tied' was his Muse by earthly powers. And Shakspere deeply felt the disgrace of being compelled to give forth his utterances in so dubious a manner.

His Sonnets [65] express the feeling that weighed upon him on this account. Had he not 'gor'd his own thoughts,' revealed his innermost soul? Yet, now, his narrow-minded fellow-dramatists--but no! not fellow-dramatists: mere contemporary playwrights, immeasurably far behind him in rank--eaten up, as they were, with envy and jealous malice, meanly derided everything sacred to him; holding up his ideals to ridicule before a jeering crowd. It has long ago been surmised that Sonnet lxvi. belongs to the 'Hamlet' period. But now it will be better understood why that sonnet speaks of 'a maiden virtue rudely strumpeted; [66] of 'right perfection wrongfully disgrac'd, and strength by limping sway disabled;' of 'simple truth miscall'd simplicity.'

These are the full words of this mighty sigh of despair:--

> Tir'd with all these, for restful death I cry--
> As, to behold desert a beggar born,
> And needy nothing trimm'd in jollity,
> And purest faith unhappily forsworn,
> And gilded honour shamefully misplac'd,

And maiden virtue rudely strumpeted,
And right perfection wrongfully disgrac'd,
And strength by limping sway disabled,
And art made tongue-ty'd by authority,
And folly (doctor-like) controlling skill,
And simple truth miscall'd simplicity,
And captive Good attending captain ill:
Tir'd with all these, from these would I be gone,
Save that, to die, I leave my love alone.

'Purest faith unhappily forsworn' was Shakspere's faith in God--without any 'holy policie' and without 'old doctrines'--trusting above all in the majesty of ennobled human nature. He was a veritable Humanist, the truest and greatest, who ever strove to raise the most essential part of human nature, man's soul and mind, yet by no mean supernatural, but by 'mean that Nature makes.'

Shakspere's 'Hamlet' appears to us like a solemn admonition to his distinguished friends. He showed them, under the guise of that Prince, a nobleman without fixed ideal--'virtues which do not go forth' to assert themselves, and to do good for the sake of others--noble life wasted, letting the world remain 'out of joint' without determined will to set it right: this was the poet's prophetic warning.

One aspiration of Shakspere clearly shines through his career, in whatever darkness it may otherwise be enveloped--namely, his longing to acquire land near the town he was born in. When he had realised this ambition, he cheerfully seems to have left the splendour of town life, and to have readily renounced all literary fame; for he did not even care to collect his own works.

He was contented to cultivate his native soil: a giant Antaeus who, as the myth tells us, ever had to touch Mother Earth to regain his strength.

Notes:

1: Volpone is stated to have been first acted in the Globe Theatre in 1605. It is simply impossible that this drama, in its present shape, should have been given in that theatre as long as Shakspere was actively connected with it. We therefore must assume that Shakspere--as Delius holds it to be probable--had at that time already withdrawn to Stratford, or that the biting allusions which are contained in Volpone against the great Master, had been added between 1605 (the year of its first performance) and 1607 (the year of its appearance in print). We consider the latter opinion the likelier one, as we suspect, from allusions in Epicoene, that Shakspere, when this play was published, still resided in London. However, it is also probable that in 1605 he may for a while have withdrawn from the stage.

2: In this enumeration, Jonson seems to have the various Qualities of the Essays in view which Florio calls 'Morall, Politike, and Millitarie.'

3: Against Montaigne, 'the teacher of things divine no less than human,' Shakspere's whole argumentation in 'Hamlet' is directed.

4: Here we have the noble Knight of the Order of St. Michael, as well as the courtier and Mayor of Bordeaux.

5: Montaigne was Knight of the Order of St. Michael, and Chamberlain of Henry III. He was on terms of friendship with Henry IV. Both Kings he had as guests in his own house. In his Essai de Vanitie, Montaigne also relates with great pride and satisfaction, that during his sojourn at Rome he was made a burgess of that city, 'the most noble that ever was, or ever shall be.'

6: In spite of Gifford's protest we do not hesitate to maintain that Jonson's Epigram LVI. (On Poet-Ape) is directed against Shakspere, and that the poet whom Jonson--in the Epistle XII. (Forest) to Elizabeth, Countess of Rutland--abuses, is also none else than Shakspere.

7: Montaigne died in 1592.

8: We can only quote the most striking points, and must leave it to the reader who takes a deeper interest in the subject, to give his own closer attention to the dramas concerning the controversy.

9: Gentlemen of Verona; Comedy of Errors; Love's Labour Lost; Love's Labour Won (probably All's Well that Ends Well); Midsummer Night's Dream; Merchant of Venice. Of Tragedies: Richard the Second; Richard the Third; Henry the Fourth; King John; Titus Andronicus; Romeo and Juliet.

10: As the words that follow seem to contain an allusion to Shakspere's Hamlet, it is to be supposed that by the 'melting heir' Jonson points to some protector of the great poet. Whether this be William Herbert, or the Earl of Southampton, we must leave undecided.

11: Act i. sc. 4.

12: Jonson probably calls Shakspere an hermaphrodite because, having a wife, he cultivated an intimate friendship at the same time with William Herbert, the later Earl of Pembroke. Jonson's Epicoene, or The Silent Woman (1609) satirises this connection. We are not the first in making this assertion. (See Sonnets of Shakspere Solved, by Henry Brown: London, 1876, p. 16.)

In Epicoene a College is described, which is stated to be composed of women. Instead of women, we may boldly assume men to be meant. Truewitt thus describes the new Society:--

'A new foundation, Sir, here in the town, of ladies, that call themselves the Collegiates: an order between courtiers and country madams that live from their husbands, and give entertainment to all the wits and braveries of the time, as they call them: cry down, or up, what they like or dislike in a brain or a fashion, with most masculine or rather hermaphroditical authority; and every day gain to their College some new probationer.

Clerimont. Who is the president?

Truewitt. The grave and youthful matron, the Lady Haughty.'
Shakspere at that time was in the 'matronly' age of forty-five.
We have seen how a 'dislike in a brain' has been expressed in Hamlet.

13: The name of Ovid, likewise used in that eulogy, Jonson assigned, in his Poetaster, to Marston. (See note 22 at end of Section V.)

14: It would have been most strange, indeed, if the two greatest geniuses of their time had not exercised some influence on each other; if the greatest thinker of that age had not given some suggestive thoughts to the poet; and if the poet had not animated the thinker to the cultivation of art, inducing him to offer his philosophical thoughts in beautiful garment. Hence Mrs. Henry Pott may have found vestiges of a more perfected and nobler style in Bacon's Diaries, on which she founded her wild theory. Had not Kant and Fichte great influence on their contemporary, Schiller? Does not Goethe praise the influence exercised by Spinoza upon him? Let us assume that the latter two had been contemporaries; that they had lived in the same town. Would it not have been extraordinary if they had remained intellectual strangers to each other, instead of drawing mutual advantage from their intercourse? Why should Bacon not have been one of the noblemen who, after the performance of a play, were initiated, in the Mermaid Tavern, into the more hidden meaning of a drama? Is it not rather likely that Bacon drew Shakspere's attention to the inconsistencies of Montaigne?

15: The advocates, in festive processions, made use of mules. Maybe that Jonson calls Shakspere a 'good dull mule' because in Hamlet he champions the views of 'Sir Lawyer' Bacon.

16: This otion, that Shakspere has mainly distinguished himself in the comic line--in the representation of Foolery--harmonises with Jonson's opinion, as privately expressed in Timber; or, Discoveries made upon Men and Matter (1630-37), in a noteworthy degree. There he says of Shakspere:--'His wit was in his own power. Would the rule of it had been so, too.'

17: An allusion to Shakspere's unclassical metrics, and his great success among the public, although in Jonson's opinion he brings neither regular 'play nor university show.'

18: In Androgyno, whom he brings in.

19: This is Jonson's answer to the question raised in Twelfth Night (act iv. sc. 2), when Malvolio is in prison, in regard to Pythagoras.

20: We can nowhere find any clue to such a personage of antiquity, and we take it to be a reference to Pyrrhon of Elis, the founder of the sceptic school.

21: Bacon was a friend of this sport. Mrs. Pott points out some technical expressions which we find both in Bacon's works and in Shakspere. Perhaps we might stretch our fancy so far as to assume that Bacon is Pyrrhus of Delos, and that gentle Shakspere sometimes went a-fishing with him on the banks of the Thames.

22: 'As itself doth relate it.' Yet the soul does not relate anything, except that it is said to have spoken, in all the characters it assumed, 'as in the cobbler's cock.' We must, therefore, probably look in plays--in Shakspere's dramas--for that which the soul has spoken in its various stages as a king, as a beggar, and so forth.

23: 'Brock' (badger)--a word which Shakspere only uses once; viz. in Twelfth Night (act ii. sc. 5). Sir Toby's whole indignation against Malvolio culminates in the words:--'Marry, hang thee, brock!' We know of Jonson's unseemly bodily figure, his 'ambling' gait, which rendered him unfit for the stage. The pace of a badger would be a very graphic description of his manner of walking. Now, Jonson sneers at the word 'brock' in a way not unfrequent with Shakspere himself, in regard to various words used by Jonson against him. In The Poetaster, Tucca falls out against the 'wormwood' comedies, which drag everything on to the stage. We are reminded here of Hamlet's exclamation:--'Wormwood, wormwood!' when the Queen of the Interlude speaks the two lines he had probably intercalated:--

In second husband let me be accurst!
None wed the second but who kill'd the first.

24: 'Cobbler's cock' refers most likely to a drama by Robert Wilson, entitled: Cobbler's Prophecy. In Collier's History of the English Drama (iii. pp. 247-8) it is thus described:--
'It is a mass of absurdity without any leading purpose, but here and there exhibiting glimpses of something better. The scene of the play is laid in Boeotia which is represented to be ruled by a duke, but in a state of confusion and disorganisation.... One of the principal characters is a whimsical Cobbler who, by intermediation of the heathen god Mercury, obtains prophetic power, the chief object of which is to warn the Duke of the impending ruin of his state unless he consents to introduce various reforms, and especially to unite the discordant classes of his subjects.' Jonson may have looked upon Hamlet in this manner from his point of view. It is for us to admire the prophetical spirit of Shakspere who in Montaigne perceived the germ of the helplessly divided nature of modern man.

25: 'Or his great oath, by Quarter.' No doubt, this is an allusion of Jonson to Shakspere's 'quarter share,' the fourth part of the receipts of his company. The Blackfriars Theatre had sixteen shareholders. It is proved that Shakspere at that time, when a valuation of the theatre was made, had a claim to four parts, each of L233 6s. 8d. (Chr. Armitage Brown, Shak. Autobiographical Poems, London, 1838, p. 101). In The Poetaster (act iii. sc. i), Tucca says to Crispinus the Poetaster:--'Thou shall have a quarter share.' In Epistle xii. (Forest), which Jonson addresses to Elizabeth, Countess of Rutland, and which, in our opinion, also contains an allusion to Shakspere, as well as to his protector, William Herbert, Ben speaks of poets with 'their quarter face.'

26: Shakspere often introduced music in his dramas. Jonson ridicules this; so did Marston, as we shall see. (Twelfth Night, for instance, opens with music.)

27: 'His golden thigh.' The shape of the legs, the 'yellow cross-gartered stockings' of poor Malvolio in Twelfth Night are here ridiculed.

28: Malvolio says to his friends:--'I am not of your element.' In the same play, great sport is made of this word, until the Fool himself at last gets weary of it, when he says (act iii. sc. i):--'You are out of my welkin--I might say element, but the word is overworn.'

29: Blackfriars, where Shakspere first acted, was a former cloister. 'On fish, when first a Carthusian I entered,' no doubt means that from the beginning he had preferred keeping mute as a fish, in regard to forbidden matters of the Church.

30: I.e., Christmas-pie. In the Prologue of The Return from Parnassus, this comedy is called a Christmas Toy. Shakspere is therein lavishly praised by his brother actors, whereas Jonson is spoken of as 'a bold whoreson, as confident now in making of a book, as he was in times past in laying of a brick.' A veritable libel!

31: Hamlet (act v. sc. 2):--

Methought, I lay
Worse than the mutines in the bilboes

32: Through Jonson's satire we always see the sanctimonious Jesuit peering out.

33: These are the parables in which Hamlet speaks. Many a reader will understand why Shakspere could not use more explicit language.

34: So the envious Jonson calls Shakspere's public who are satisfied with 'salad;' that is, with patchy compositions, pieced together from all kinds of material.

35: Jonson had Scottish ancestry.

36: In a moment of fanaticism, Hamlet wishes Ophelia to go to a nunnery. Jonson, in most cynical manner, means to say that Hamlet had been impotent as regards his innamorata. Though 'for the nones' may be taken as 'for the nonce,' it yet comes close enough to a double-entendre--namely, 'for the nuns.'

37: Dramatic versus Wit Combats. London, 1864. Ed. John Russell Smith.

38: To mount a bank = mountebank.

39: From one of them poor Ben received a vile medicine: a purge.

40: 'Lewd'=unlearned.

41: Shakspere's Autobiographical Poems.

42: Karl Elze (Essays on Shakespeare; London 1874) thinks this passage is intended against Shakespeare's alleged theft committed in the Tempest, the composition of which he, therefore, places in the year 1604-5, while most critics assign it to a much later period. It must also be mentioned that Karl Elze draws attention to the more friendly words with which Jonson, in his own handwriting, dedicates his Volpone to Florio.
In the opinion of the German critic, it is not difficult to gather from this Dedication the desire of the meanly quarrelsome scholar Jonson to give his friend Florio to understand that, among other things, he would read with considerable satisfaction how he (Jonson) had made short work with this 'Shake-scene' and this 'upstart Crow.'

43: Dekker tells Horace that his--Johnson's--plays are misliked at Court. According to the above-quoted words of Jonson, Hamlet seems to have pleased at Court on its first appearance.

44: The following passage in Jonson's Epicoene is also interesting, though in the play itself it is not made to refer to Montaigne but apparently to Plutarch and Seneca: 'Grave asses! mere essayists: a few loose sentences, and that's all. A man could talk so his whole age. I do utter as good things every hour if they were collected and observed, as either of them.' May not such words have fallen from Shakspere's lips, in regard to Montaigne, before an intimate circle in the Mermaid Tavern?

45: This may point either to Montaigne or to Dr. Guinne, the fellow-worker of Florio in the translation of the Essays, whom the latter calls 'a monster-quelling Theseus or Hercules.'

46: The reasons which induce us to this opinion are the following: The three authors of Eastward Hoe were arrested on account of a satire contained in this play against the Scots; James I., himself a Scot, having become King of England a year before. The audacious stage-poets were threatened with having their noses and ears cut off. They were presently freed, however; probably through the intervention of some noblemen. Soon afterwards, Jonson was again in prison; and we suspect that this second imprisonment took place in consequence of Volpone. We base this view on several incidents. In a letter Jonson addressed in 1605, from his place of confinement, to Lord Salisbury (Ben Jonson, edited by Cunningham, vol. i. xlix.), he says that he regrets having once more to apply to his kindness on account of a play, after having scarcely repented 'his first error' (most probably Eastward Hoe).' Before I can shew myself grateful in the least for former benefits, I am enforced to provoke your bounties for more.' In this letter, Jonson uses a tone similar to the one which pervades his Dedication of Volpone. We therefore believe that both letter and Dedication have reference to one and the same matter. In the letter, Jonson addresses Lord Salisbury in this way:--'My noble lord, they deal not charitably who are witty in another man's work, and utter sometimes their own malicious meanings under our words.' He then continues, protesting that since his first error, which was punished more with his shame than with his bondage, he has only touched at general vice, sparing particular persons. He goes on:--'I beseech your most honourable Lordship, suffer not other men's errors or faults past to be made my crimes; but let me be examined by all my works past and this present; and trust not to Rumour, but my books (for she is an unjust deliverer, both of great and of small actions), whether I have ever (many things I have written private and public) given offence to a nation, to a public order or state, or any person of honour or authority; but have equally laboured to keep their dignity, as my own person, safe.'

Now, let us compare the following verses from the second Prologue of Epicoene (the plural here becomes the singular):--
  If any yet will, with particular sleight
  Of application, (Occasioned by some person's impertinent
  Exceptions.)
  wrest what he doth write;
  And that he meant, or him, or her, will say:
  They make a libel, which he made a play.
Nor will it be easy to find out who was the cause of Volpone having been persecuted at one time--that is to say, forbidden to be acted on the stage. (Perchance by the 'obstreperous Sir Lawyer' who is mentioned in it?)
We direct the reader's attention to the eulogistic poems composed by Jonson's friends on Volpone. (Ben Jonson, by Cunningham, vol. i. pp. civ.-cv.) First there are the extraordinary praises written by those who sign their names in full:--J. DONNE, E. BOLTON, FRANCIS BEAUMONT. Then follow verses, probably composed somewhat later, which are cautiously signed by initials only--D. D., J. C., G. C., E. S., J. F., T. R. This is not the case with any other eulogistic poems referring to Jonson's dramas. The verses before mentioned, which are only signed by initials, all speak of a 'persecuted fox, or of a fox killed by hounds.'

47: 'Come, my coach!' means: 'I value my honour less than my coach.' The expression, 'O, how the wheel becomes it!' is of such a character that we must refer the reader to Montaigne's Essay III. 11.

48: Eastward Hoe< was acted in the Blackfriars Theatre by 'The Children of Her Majestie's Revels.'

49: Until now it has been assumed that The Malcontent was acted by Shakspere's Company in the Globe Theatre. This conclusion was based on the title-page of the drama, which runs thus:--
  THE MALCONTENT
  Augmented by Marston
  With the Additions played by the Kings

MAIESTIES SERVANTS
Written
by JOHN WEBSTER.

It is, however, to be noted that in regard to all other plays of Marston, whenever it is mentioned by whom they were acted (so, for instance, in regard to The Parasitaster, the Dutch Courtesane, and Eastward Hoe), the title is always indicated in this way (designating both the Theatre and the Company):--'As it was plaid in the Black Friars by the Children of her Maiesties Revels.' Again, the mere perusal of the 'Induction' of The Malcontent (not to speak of the drama itself) shows that this play could not have been acted 'by the Kings Maiesties servants' during Shakspere's membership. For, in this Induction there appear four actors of Shakspere's company: Sly, Burbadge, Condell, and Lowin. They are brought in to justify themselves why they act a certain play, 'another Company having interest in it.' One of the actors excuses their doing so by saying that, as they themselves have been similarly robbed, they have a clear right to Malevole, the chief character in The Malcontent. 'Why not Malevole in folio with us, as Jeronimo in decimo sexto with them? They taught us a name for our play: we call it: "One for Another."' (That is to say, we give them 'Tit for Tat.')

  Sly. What are your additions?

  Burbadge. Sooth, not greatly needefull, only as your sallet (salad) to your greate feast--to entertaine a little more time, and to abridge the not received custome of musicke in our theater. I must leave you, Sir. [Exit Burbadge.

  Sinklow. Doth he play The Malcontent?

  Condell. Yes, Sir.

Our explanation of the Induction is this: Marston has committed satirical trespass upon Hamlet. Shakspere, on his part, made use of the chief action and the chief characters of The Malcontent in his Measure for Measure ('One for Another'); but he did so in his own nobler manner. From the wildly confused material before him he composed a magnificent drama. Once more, in the very beginning of act i. sc. I, Shakspere makes the Duke utter words, each of which is directed against the inactive nature of Montaigne:--

  Thyself and thy belongings
  Are not thine own so proper as to waste
  Thyself upon thy virtues, them on thee.
  ...For if our virtues
  Did not go forth of us, 't were all alike
  As if we had them not.

Shakspere's contemporaries were not over careful as regards style. 'With the additions played by the Kings Maiesties Servants, written by John Webster,' means that the additions, in which the servants of His Majesty, in the 'Induction,' are brought on the stage, were written by John Webster.

Read the 'Extempore Prologue' which Sly speaks at the conclusion of the Induction--a shameless travesty of the Epilogue in As You Like It. Read the beginning of act iii. sc. 2 of The Malcontent, where Malevole ('in some freeze gown') burlesques the splendid monologue in King Henry the Fourth (Part 11. act iv. sc. I). Read act iii. sc. 3 of The Malcontent, where Marston sneers at the scene in act iv. of King Richard the Second when Richard says:--

  Now is this golden crown like a deep well,
  That owes two buckets filling one another.

50: Is it imaginable that Shakspere could have allowed his own most beautiful productions to be thus leered at, and mocked, in his own theatre? Our feeling rebels against the thought.

  Beniamini Jonsonio
  Poetae Elegantissimo Gravissimo
  Amico Suo Candido et Cordato
  Johannes Marston, Musarum Alumnus,
  Asperam Hanc Suam Thaliam DD.

51: Who else can be meant by the 'Frenchman's Helicon' than Montaigne? He is satirically called 'Helicon,' as he is taken down from his height in 'Hamlet.'
52: In meaning alike to Jonson's: 'Counting all old doctrine heresie.'
53: Act i. sc.2.
54: Act iv. sc. 5.
55: Act i. sc. 4.
56: Act i. sc. 7.
57: Act i. sc. 6.
58: Act iii. sc. 2.
59: Act ii. sc. 5.
60: Act i. Sc. 5 in Hamlet; Malcontent, act iii. sc. 3.
61: Perhaps an allusion to the conclusion of Hamlet, when the State falls into the hands of a soldier (Fortinbras). --Soldaten-Religion, keine Religion ('a soldier's religion, no religion'), as the old German saying is.
62: Rochelle-Churchman--that is, Huguenot.
63: See Bacon's Essay, Of Atheism: 'All that impugn a received religion or superstition are by the adverse part branded with the name of Atheists.'
64: Sonnet lxvi. lxxxv.
65: xc. xci. xcii.
66: In Eastward Hoe, his most delicate poetical production, Ophelia, is most abominably parodied--'rudely strumpeted.'

www.bookjungle.com *email: sales@bookjungle.com fax: 630-214-0564 mail: Book Jungle PO Box 2226 Champaign, IL 61825*

The Codes Of Hammurabi And Moses
W. W. Davies

QTY

The discovery of the Hammurabi Code is one of the greatest achievements of archaeology, and is of paramount interest, not only to the student of the Bible, but also to all those interested in ancient history...

Religion   **ISBN:** *1-59462-338-4*   Pages:132
                                              MSRP $12.95

The Theory of Moral Sentiments
Adam Smith

QTY

This work from 1749. contains original theories of conscience amd moral judgment and it is the foundation for systemof morals.

Philosophy   **ISBN:** *1-59462-777-0*   Pages:536
                                              MSRP $19.95

Jessica's First Prayer
Hesba Stretton

QTY

In a screened and secluded corner of one of the many railway-bridges which span the streets of London there could be seen a few years ago, from five o'clock every morning until half past eight, a tidily set-out coffee-stall, consisting of a trestle and board, upon which stood two large tin cans, with a small fire of charcoal burning under each so as to keep the coffee boiling during the early hours of the morning when the work-people were thronging into the city on their way to their daily toil...

Childrens   **ISBN:** *1-59462-373-2*   Pages:84
                                              MSRP $9.95

My Life and Work
Henry Ford

QTY

Henry Ford revolutionized the world with his implementation of mass production for the Model T automobile. Gain valuable business insight into his life and work with his own auto-biography... "We have only started on our development of our country we have not as yet, with all our talk of wonderful progress, done more than scratch the surface. The progress has been wonderful enough but..."

Biographies/ **ISBN:** *1-59462-198-5*   **Pages:300**
                                              MSRP $21.95

www.bookjungle.com email: sales@bookjungle.com fax: 630-214-0564 mail: Book Jungle PO Box 2226 Champaign, IL 61825

The Art of Cross-Examination
Francis Wellman

QTY

I presume it is the experience of every author, after his first book is published upon an important subject, to be almost overwhelmed with a wealth of ideas and illustrations which could readily have been included in his book, and which to his own mind, at least, seem to make a second edition inevitable. Such certainly was the case with me; and when the first edition had reached its sixth impression in five months, I rejoiced to learn that it seemed to my publishers that the book had met with a sufficiently favorable reception to justify a second and considerably enlarged edition. ...

Reference   ISBN: *1-59462-647-2*

Pages:412
MSRP *$19.95*

On the Duty of Civil Disobedience
Henry David Thoreau

QTY

Thoreau wrote his famous essay, On the Duty of Civil Disobedience, as a protest against an unjust but popular war and the immoral but popular institution of slave-owning. He did more than write—he declined to pay his taxes, and was hauled off to gaol in consequence. Who can say how much this refusal of his hastened the end of the war and of slavery ?

Law   ISBN: *1-59462-747-9*

Pages:48
MSRP *$7.45*

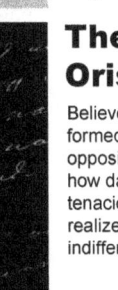

Dream Psychology Psychoanalysis for Beginners
Sigmund Freud

QTY

Sigmund Freud, born Sigismund Schlomo Freud (May 6, 1856 - September 23, 1939), was a Jewish-Austrian neurologist and psychiatrist who co-founded the psychoanalytic school of psychology. Freud is best known for his theories of the unconscious mind, especially involving the mechanism of repression; his redefinition of sexual desire as mobile and directed towards a wide variety of objects; and his therapeutic techniques, especially his understanding of transference in the therapeutic relationship and the presumed value of dreams as sources of insight into unconscious desires.

Psychology   ISBN: *1-59462-905-6*

Pages:196
MSRP *$15.45*

The Miracle of Right Thought
Orison Swett Marden

QTY

Believe with all of your heart that you will do what you were made to do. When the mind has once formed the habit of holding cheerful, happy, prosperous pictures, it will not be easy to form the opposite habit. It does not matter how improbable or how far away this realization may see, or how dark the prospects may be, if we visualize them as best we can, as vividly as possible, hold tenaciously to them and vigorously struggle to attain them, they will gradually become actualized, realized in the life. But a desire, a longing without endeavor, a yearning abandoned or held indifferently will vanish without realization.

Self Help   ISBN: *1-59462-644-8*

Pages:360
MSRP *$25.45*

www.bookjungle.com email: sales@bookjungle.com fax: 630-214-0564 mail: Book Jungle PO Box 2226 Champaign, IL 61825

QTY

The Rosicrucian Cosmo-Conception Mystic Christianity by *Max Heindel* ISBN: *1-59462-188-8* **$38.95**
The Rosicrucian Cosmo-conception is not dogmatic, neither does it appeal to any other authority than the reason of the student. It is: not controversial, but is: sent forth in the, hope that it may help to clear...
New Age/Religion Pages 646

Abandonment To Divine Providence by *Jean-Pierre de Caussade* ISBN: *1-59462-228-0* **$25.95**
"The Rev. Jean Pierre de Caussade was one of the most remarkable spiritual writers of the Society of Jesus in France in the 18th Century. His death took place at Toulouse in 1751. His works have gone through many editions and have been republished..."
Inspirational/Religion Pages 400

Mental Chemistry by *Charles Haanel* ISBN: *1-59462-192-6* **$23.95**
Mental Chemistry allows the change of material conditions by combining and appropriately utilizing the power of the mind. Much like applied chemistry creates something new and unique out of careful combinations of chemicals the mastery of mental chemistry...
New Age/Business Pages 354

The Letters of Robert Browning and Elizabeth Barret Barrett 1845-1846 vol II ISBN: *1-59462-193-4* **$35.95**
by *Robert Browning* and *Elizabeth Barrett*
Biographies Pages 596

Gleanings In Genesis (volume I) by *Arthur W. Pink* ISBN: *1-59462-130-6* **$27.45**
Appropriately has Genesis been termed "the seed plot of the Bible" for in it we have, in germ form, almost all of the great doctrines which are afterwards fully developed in the books of Scripture which follow...
Religion/Inspirational Pages 420

The Master Key by *L. W. de Laurence* ISBN: *1-59462-001-6* **$30.95**
In no branch of human knowledge has there been a more lively increase of the spirit of research during the past few years than in the study of Psychology, Concentration and Mental Discipline. The requests for authentic lessons in Thought Control, Mental Discipline and...
New Age/Business Pages 422

The Lesser Key Of Solomon Goetia by *L. W. de Laurence* ISBN: *1-59462-092-X* **$9.95**
This translation of the first book of the "Lemegton" which is now for the first time made accessible to students of Talismanic Magic was done, after careful collation and edition, from numerous Ancient Manuscripts in Hebrew, Latin, and French...
New Age/Occult Pages 92

Rubaiyat Of Omar Khayyam by *Edward Fitzgerald* ISBN: *1-59462-332-5* **$13.95**
Edward Fitzgerald, whom the world has already learned, in spite of his own efforts to remain within the shadow of anonymity, to look upon as one of the rarest poets of the century, was born at Bredfield, in Suffolk, on the 31st of March, 1809. He was the third son of John Purcell...
Music Pages 172

Ancient Law by *Henry Maine* ISBN: *1-59462-128-4* **$29.95**
The chief object of the following pages is to indicate some of the earliest ideas of mankind, as they are reflected in Ancient Law, and to point out the relation of those ideas to modern thought.
Religiom/History Pages 452

Far-Away Stories by *William J. Locke* ISBN: *1-59462-129-2* **$19.45**
"Good wine needs no bush, but a collection of mixed vintages does. And this book is just such a collection. Some of the stories I do not want to remain buried for ever in the museum files of dead magazine-numbers an author's not unpardonable vanity..."
Fiction Pages 272

Life of David Crockett by *David Crockett* ISBN: *1-59462-250-7* **$27.45**
"Colonel David Crockett was one of the most remarkable men of the times in which he lived. Born in humble life, but gifted with a strong will, an indomitable courage, and unremitting perseverance...
Biographies/New Age Pages 424

Lip-Reading by *Edward Nitchie* ISBN: *1-59462-206-X* **$25.95**
Edward B. Nitchie, founder of the New York School for the Hard of Hearing, now the Nitchie School of Lip-Reading, Inc, wrote "LIP-READING Principles and Practice". The development and perfecting of this meritorious work on lip-reading was an undertaking...
How-to Pages 400

A Handbook of Suggestive Therapeutics, Applied Hypnotism, Psychic Science ISBN: *1-59462-214-0* **$24.95**
by *Henry Munro*
Health/New Age/Health/Self-help Pages 376

A Doll's House: and Two Other Plays by *Henrik Ibsen* ISBN: *1-59462-112-8* **$19.95**
Henrik Ibsen created this classic when in revolutionary 1848 Rome. Introducing some striking concepts in playwriting for the realist genre, this play has been studied the world over.
Fiction/Classics/Plays 308

The Light of Asia by *sir Edwin Arnold* ISBN: *1-59462-204-3* **$13.95**
In this poetic masterpiece, Edwin Arnold describes the life and teachings of Buddha. The man who was to become known as Buddha to the world was born as Prince Gautama of India but he rejected the worldly riches and abandoned the reigns of power when...
Religion/History/Biographies Pages 170

The Complete Works of Guy de Maupassant by *Guy de Maupassant* ISBN: *1-59462-157-8* **$16.95**
"For days and days, nights and nights, I had dreamed of that first kiss which was to consecrate our engagement, and I knew not on what spot I should put my lips..."
Fiction/Classics Pages 240

The Art of Cross-Examination by *Francis L. Wellman* ISBN: *1-59462-309-0* **$26.95**
Written by a renowned trial lawyer, Wellman imparts his experience and uses case studies to explain how to use psychology to extract desired information through questioning.
How-to/Science/Reference Pages 408

Answered or Unanswered? by *Louisa Vaughan* ISBN: *1-59462-248-5* **$10.95**
Miracles of Faith in China
Religion Pages 112

The Edinburgh Lectures on Mental Science (1909) by *Thomas* ISBN: *1-59462-008-3* **$11.95**
This book contains the substance of a course of lectures recently given by the writer in the Queen Street Hall, Edinburgh. Its purpose is to indicate the Natural Principles governing the relation between Mental Action and Material Conditions...
New Age/Psychology Pages 148

Ayesha by *H. Rider Haggard* ISBN: *1-59462-301-5* **$24.95**
Verily and indeed it is the unexpected that happens! Probably if there was one person upon the earth from whom the Editor of this, and of a certain previous history, did not expect to hear again...
Classics Pages 380

Ayala's Angel by *Anthony Trollope* ISBN: *1-59462-352-X* **$29.95**
The two girls were both pretty, but Lucy who was twenty-one who supposed to be simple and comparatively unattractive, whereas Ayala was credited, as her Bombwhat romantic name might show, with poetic charm and a taste for romance. Ayala when her father died was nineteen...
Fiction Pages 484

The American Commonwealth by *James Bryce* ISBN: *1-59462-286-8* **$34.45**
An interpretation of American democratic political theory. It examines political mechanics and society from the perspective of Scotsman James Bryce
Politics Pages 572

Stories of the Pilgrims by *Margaret P. Pumphrey* ISBN: *1-59462-116-0* **$17.95**
This book explores pilgrims religious oppression in England as well as their escape to Holland and eventual crossing to America on the Mayflower, and their early days in New England...
History Pages 268

www.bookjungle.com email: sales@bookjungle.com fax: 630-214-0564 mail: Book Jungle PO Box 2226 Champaign, IL 61825

QTY

The Fasting Cure by *Sinclair Upton* ISBN: *1-59462-222-1* **$13.95**
In the Cosmopolitan Magazine for May, 1910, and in the Contemporary Review (London) for April, 1910, I published an article dealing with my experiences in fasting. I have written a great many magazine articles, but never one which attracted so much attention... *New Age/Self Help/Health Pages 164*

Hebrew Astrology by *Sepharial* ISBN: *1-59462-308-2* **$13.45**
In these days of advanced thinking it is a matter of common observation that we have left many of the old landmarks behind and that we are now pressing forward to greater heights and to a wider horizon than that which represented the mind-content of our progenitors... *Astrology Pages 144*

Thought Vibration or The Law of Attraction in the Thought World ISBN: *1-59462-127-6* **$12.95**
by *William Walker Atkinson* *Psychology/Religion Pages 144*

Optimism by *Helen Keller* ISBN: *1-59462-108-X* **$15.95**
Helen Keller was blind, deaf, and mute since 19 months old, yet famously learned how to overcome these handicaps, communicate with the world, and spread her lectures promoting optimism. An inspiring read for everyone... *Biographies/Inspirational Pages 84*

Sara Crewe by *Frances Burnett* ISBN: *1-59462-360-0* **$9.45**
In the first place, Miss Minchin lived in London. Her home was a large, dull, tall one, in a large, dull square, where all the houses were alike, and all the sparrows were alike, and where all the door-knockers made the same heavy sound... *Childrens/Classic Pages 88*

The Autobiography of Benjamin Franklin by *Benjamin Franklin* ISBN: *1-59462-135-7* **$24.95**
The Autobiography of Benjamin Franklin has probably been more extensively read than any other American historical work, and no other book of its kind has had such ups and downs of fortune. Franklin lived for many years in England, where he was agent... *Biographies/History Pages 332*

Name	
Email	
Telephone	
Address	
City, State ZIP	

☐ Credit Card   ☐ Check / Money Order

Credit Card Number	
Expiration Date	
Signature	

Please Mail to: Book Jungle
PO Box 2226
Champaign, IL 61825
or Fax to: 630-214-0564

ORDERING INFORMATION

web: *www.bookjungle.com*
email: *sales@bookjungle.com*
fax: *630-214-0564*
mail: *Book Jungle PO Box 2226 Champaign, IL 61825*
or PayPal *to sales@bookjungle.com*

Please contact us for bulk discounts

DIRECT-ORDER TERMS

**20% Discount if You Order
Two or More Books**
Free Domestic Shipping!
Accepted: Master Card, Visa,
Discover, American Express

www.ingramcontent.com/pod-product-compliance
Lightning Source LLC
Chambersburg PA
CBHW080503110426
42742CB00017B/2986